TAWNY, THE MAGNIFICENT JAGUAR

and Other Great Jungle Stories

Compiled and edited by
Joe L. Wheeler

PACIFIC PRESS® PUBLISHING ASSOCIATION
NAMPA, IDAHO
OSHAWA, ONTARIO, CANADA
WWW.PACIFICPRESS.COM

Cover art by Lars Justinen
Cover designed by Justinen Creative Group
Interior illustrations from the library of Joe L. Wheeler
Inside design by Aaron Troia

Copyright © 2012 by
Pacific Press® Publishing Association
Printed in the United States of America

The author assumes full responsibility for the accuracy of all facts and quotations as cited
in this book.

Additional copies of this book are available by calling toll-free 1-800-765-6955 or by
visiting www.adventistbookcenter.com.

www.joewheelerbooks.com

Representing the author is WordServe Literary Group Ltd., 10152 Knoll Circle, Highland
Ranch, CO 80130.

Library of Congress Cataloging-in-Publication Data:

Tawny, the Magnificent Jaguar and Other Great Jungle Stories / compiled and
edited by Joe L. Wheeler.
p. cm.
ISBN 13: 978-0-8163-2533-7 (pbk.)
ISBN 10: 0-8163-2533-2 (pbk.)

1. Animals—Anecdotes. I. Wheeler, Joe L., 1936-

QL791.T27 2012
591—dc23

2011039919

12 13 14 15 16 • 5 4 3 2 1

DEDICATION

Such an integral part of my growing-up years in Latin America was she—and impossible to ever forget!—that this book of jungle stories is dedicated to my irrepressible gadabout parrot:

LORITA

Left to Right: Joe and Lorita, Barbara, Romayne, and Lawrence Wheeler in Guatemala City.

Other books in the series
The Good Lord Made Them All
by Joe L. Wheeler

Amelia, the Flying Squirrel
and Other Great Stories of God's Smallest Creatures

Dick, the Babysitting Bear
and Other Great Wild Animal Stories

Owney, the Post Office Dog
and Other Great Dog Stories

Smoky, the Ugliest Cat in the World
and Other Great Cat Stories

Spot, the Dog That Broke the Rules
and Other Great Heroic Animal Stories

Togo, the Sled Dog
and Other Great Animal Stories of the North

Wildfire, the Red Stallion
and Other Great Horse Stories

Contents

INTRODUCTION

NO ESCAPE ANYWHERE

Joseph Leininger Wheeler

There is something about stories featuring animals with larger-than-life reputations, such as rhinos, elephants, buffaloes, lions, tigers, leopards, jaguars, and serpents, that fascinate not only children but all age groups. What could be more terrifying than a man-eating tiger on the prowl or a rampaging rogue elephant? Thus this collection of stories has its place in this The Good Lord Made Them All series of books. Another portion of God's great "Web of Life."

* * * * *

How true it is that in the jungle, there is no escape anywhere. Almost every animal, it seems, has a nemesis that it fears. That so-called king of the beasts, the lion, fears the cape buffalo, the elephant, and marauding packs of jackals; the tiger fears the leopard and the elephant; the elephant fears most of all the nasty-dispositioned rhinoceros, whose one joy in life appears to be goring most any animal that comes into view (however, the elephant usually wins). Even the king cobra (so feared by both man and beast) dreads the sight of that weasel-like little animal, the mongoose.

But this survival of the fittest is not unique to just jungle animals; it is true of virtually the entire animal kingdom, no matter in what part of the world, climate, or environment they may find themselves.

First of all, though, for the purposes of this particular story collection, let's define what a jungle is or is not. I don't know about you, but I've always assumed that a jungle was, quite simply, an extremely dense tropical thicket. Well, it is, and it isn't.

According to the editors of the Random House unabridged *Dictionary of the English Language*, the first definition of *jungle* confirms what I always thought it was: "A wild land overgrown with dense vegetation, often nearly impenetrable, especially tropical vegetation or a tropical rain forest."

But the definition does not stop there, it also includes a list of variants:

"A wilderness of dense undergrowth."
"A piece of swampy, thick-set forest land."
"A scene of violence and struggle for survival."
"A place or situation of ruthless competition."

According to these four definitions, almost any environment harboring animal life—or even insect life—could be aptly named a "jungle." Nevertheless, for this particular collection of jungle stories, I am excluding oceanic animals and animals of the North.

This is the first book in the series that is truly global, featuring, as it does, animals from Mexico, Guatemala, El Salvador, Nicaragua, Honduras, Costa Rica, Jamaica, Peru, Ecuador, Colombia, Brazil, South Africa, Seychelles islands, Kenya, Algeria, Egypt, Thailand, Myanmar, India, and Australia.

In recent years it has become fashionable, especially in the West, to gloss over harsh realities with euphemisms. Most of all, anything having to do with death. Rather than admit someone actually died, we resort to euphemisms such as, "passed away," "went to his reward," "shuffled off this mortal coil," "ceased to breathe," "gave up the ghost"—oh, the list goes on and on.

Yet, death is rarely pretty. If we deny the reality of death to our children, for instance, how are they then to understand death when it comes to someone near and dear to them?

Just so, to prevaricate to our children about the continual "survival of the fittest" going on all about them is to set them up for disillusionment and cynicism when they discover the truth. When they discover that virtually

every nondomesticated animal fixates on (1) the struggle to stay alive; (2) the struggle to get enough food (and most are carnivores rather than vegetarians); (3) the struggle involved in having to continually attack to stay alive, or having to continually defend to stay alive; and (4) and the universal instinct to procreate.

Consequently, a collection of jungle stories such as this can serve as a useful learning tool where grandparents, parents, and children can interact, discussing these realities taking place around them every day.

Christians, of course, are able to enter into discussions that result in understandable answers: that the "survival of the fittest" is one of the most significant results of the Fall in the Garden of Eden. And that it will remain so until the earth is made new.

Whatever one's religion or philosophy of life might be, it is a fact of life that no child will be satisfied until provided with reasons for the "survival of the fittest" that make some sort of logical sense to them.

CODA

I look forward to hearing from you! I always welcome the stories, responses, and suggestions that are sent to us from our readers. I am putting together collections centered on other genres as well. You may reach me by writing to:

Joe L. Wheeler, PhD
P.O. Box 1246
Conifer, CO 80433

* * * * *

TAWNY

Edith Bowden

How could Tawny and Golden Fur have known that there were some kinds of animals that were off-limits to jaguars.

Then the dogs were upon them, followed by men on horseback carrying sticks that gleamed in the sun and spouted fire.

By then it looked hopeless . . .

* * * *

Hunting hounds! Only a pack on the hot scent could blare out that fear-inspiring cry. The threatening sound made the little yellow deer and the coatis scuttle deeper into the tropical forest.

A pair of great spotted jaguars, dozing under a *quebracho* tree in a lonely Mato Grosso valley not far from the edge of the Brazilian jungle, merely opened and closed their drowsy eyes.

The approaching battle cry of the pack finally awakened the golden beasts. Slowly they raised their heads to glance toward a distant spot in the north where a few straggling wild cattle grazed.

As the din increased, Tawny nuzzled his mate. He wanted consolation for being disturbed. He hated being aroused when he was resting after a meal.

At last he rose to stretch himself. A yawn grew into a rumble of annoyance.

Golden Fur's thoughts were centered on something strange in their well-known surroundings. The sight of the long-horned wild cattle kicking up their heels to dash off westward to the Tapajos River first made her suspicious. When she pointed her velvety nozzle to the wind, she smelled an unfamiliar scent.

Tawny showed no alarm. Why should he? He was not afraid. The great three-hundred-pound cat had never in his life met anything that he could not conquer. He stretched—stretched until the powerful muscles rippled under his tawny pelt.

Steadily the clamor increased. Fearlessly the jaguar strolled forward at the sight of unfamiliar objects coming toward him—men on horseback surrounded by dogs. The party stopped at the half-eaten carcass of a bull Tawny had recently killed.

All at once Golden Fur nudged her mate in the flank. When he did not budge, she snapped at him gently. Still Tawny the Magnificent refused to heed her warning. Still he lingered, even though a strong odor of man scent came sweeping down the wind. Because it had never crossed his path before, nothing within him warned him that these were his natural enemies.

His mate was wiser, however, for she felt instinctively that the intruders boded ill for jaguars. The bows and arrows and the glint of the solitary shiny rifle, as well as the dog howls, all combined to make her tingle with fearful excitement.

As the cavalcade came closer, Golden Fur punched Tawny hard as if to say, "How can you be so stupid!" But the king of cats had not the slightest premonition of their impending fate!

The intruders moved in a circle-swing to place themselves between the jaguars and the jungle, proceeding with a casualness that seemed to Golden Fur to show an evil definiteness. She sensed blindly that their coming would at least make it harder for the jaguars to eat.

Golden Fur had known what it was to be hungry. She and Tawny had been gaunt for lack of food. Their hunger had driven them far, far inland through a maze of forest; had brought them through the jungle and into this isolated section where they had found great droves of half-wild cattle.

All at once Golden Fur heard Tawny blast an ugly noise. She looked up to see a flurry of dog bodies streaking straight from the east.

Then with a vicious snarl, Tawny awaited the pack. The wild wish to flee almost overpowered the female, but she knew that Tawny would not run. Thus, with never a thought of deserting her mate, Golden Fur bounded to her rightful place at his side.

The pair had been together ever since the day when Tawny had first seen her come down to a stream to drink. He had been a good mate and a good provider of food. Golden Fur had done her share too. She, not Tawny, had always caught all their fish.

The great male hated rivers. He loathed them. He would never go into a stream, for he had a horror of the vicious *jacarés* (a kind of crocodile) and the man-eating little piranha fish that crowded to the surface at the taste and the smell of blood. He felt much less afraid of land enemies—even large and strange ones like these new invaders that were bearing swiftly down upon him.

As the pair of jungle cats faced the oncoming attackers, the great male spread his paws to get a firmer grip. A feeling akin to delight seized him as he saw his foremost enemy. Only an untrained dog would approach close to a full-grown jaguar.

Even as this thought flashed through Tawny's mind, the great male was surprised.

The hound changed his tactics suddenly. He zigzagged sharply; and openly abandoning his pretense of fighting Tawny, he dived straight for Golden Fur. Perhaps he expected to kill her. Perhaps he expected only to nip her and then dash back, luring Tawny to the pack.

This act of rashness cost the hound his life. With a deafening roar, Tawny bared his yellow fangs; then he flung his massive frame in front of his mate. At the same time he lunged out with a death-dealing paw.

There was a wild cry. The dog rolled over to lie quiet, his back broken by the blow.

After a second of silence, the fight was on. Wild confusion sounded across the plain. It was as if a relentless tornado had swept down upon the jaguars.

Excited horsemen yelled at their dogs and spurred their horses forward. The spearmen and the archers leaped to the ground and tested their weapons, while the only hunter with a rifle rode up closer and closer.

The jaguars growled and leaped, charging the dogs. Then they retreated to be in a position to charge again. Golden Fur's armored claws slashed a luckless terrier, and once she sprang in a curve to land on a mongrel, crushing him to the ground.

A babel of battle sounds echoed across the grassland. The dark-skinned Brazilian spearmen shrieked at their dogs, first encouraging them, then scolding them. They ordered the hounds to fight, and in the same breath they ordered them to stop fighting. They yelled at the spotted cats for killing the hunting pack, and they raged at the pack for blocking their spears and arrows.

Horses neighed. Mules brayed. Suddenly the hunter with the rifle urged his horse forward until it snorted with terror. He did not even wait for the hounds to bring the great cat to bay, but raised the old-style rifle to his shoulder.

All at once, just as there came a split-second lull in the fight, he pulled the trigger. A spurt of flame! A roar! Then something whizzed so close to Tawny's head that he could hear the bullet sing.

The great cat dropped on his stomach. As he crouched, he had a momentary pang of fear. For the first time in his life, he felt the urge to flee from his enemy. He swung round swiftly. With the faintest signal to Golden Fur, he was off like a rocket. He knew she would be running at his side.

Five seconds later, his mate was bounding over the grassy hillocks behind the speeding Tawny. The baying hounds followed, keeping a safe distance at her heels. The hunters scrambled for their mounts, some of the riders sweeping in behind the dogs, and others racing along on the left flank.

With leaping sweeps, Golden Fur gained on her mate as he turned due east and headed for the jungle. There lay safety.

The jaguars were splendid runners. They settled into a springy flight, running in graceful sweeps as they traveled with tremendous speed. There was as yet no panic in their hearts, as yet no fear that they were racing to their doom.

Slowly Golden Fur gained on Tawny as he loped away from the Tapajos River. At last they were running almost neck and neck. The great male cat was glad they were headed away from the river. He was glad that the chase led toward the jungle.

Although the forest was a network of vines and undergrowth, the jaguars were not afraid to dash into it. The two great cats knew the aisles that opened off the entering lanes.

The chase swept on, the jaguars skimming over the ground with mighty flying leaps. At the end of the first mile, the great cats had a big lead; but the hounds and the hunters were crowding them away from the jungle.

At the end of the second mile, Tawny could hear more plainly the cries of the dogs and the shouts of the hunters. At the end of the third mile, Tawny and his mate still held the lead. Whenever the dogs gained any ground, the jaguars miraculously increased their speeds.

As the hunted pair passed by the opening out of which months ago they had emerged into this grassland, Tawny caught a flying glimpse of it. How lucky they had been since then!

How could the pair have known that they were courting death by their wanton slaughter of the herd! Their waste of meat had been so brazen that the smaller animals had long since learned to follow them to eat the food they left.

Since Tawny was quite ignorant of human beings, he could not know that men had seen him and spread great tales about him. He did not know that men had said he was destructive.

As the great male's breath came faster, he ran less swiftly. Glancing around occasionally, he assured himself that the dogs were no longer gaining on him. Tawny's heart pounded with anticipation when he approached a spot within less than a mile of the jungle fringe. It was not an instant too soon, either, for Golden Fur's breath was coming in gasps. He slackened his pace, loath to appear to leave her.

Just as the painted pair caught a welcome whiff of the pungent eucalyptus tree that marked the hidden jungle entrance they were planning to enter, Tawny's quivering nostrils caught a faint trace of something else—the dreaded man scent! He did not need to see the group of native hunters half hidden in the underbrush to know that all was lost!

Golden Fur did not whimper once in the second that it took Tawny to decide whether they should veer north or south. She heard the ringing cry of the fresh pack.

Together the panting creatures ran parallel to the jungle. Could they outdistance the hounds in the desperate game? The formation of the chase had shaped itself into the letter V, with the jaguars at the point and the bands of pursuing hounds at the opposite ends.

The fresh hunters marveled that the spotted beasts appeared able to draw upon some unexpected supply of strength in their frenzied efforts to reach the forest.

Craftily the hounds forced them back—back—back upon the grasslands. The jaguars, traveling first parallel to the jungle and then running back toward the east, zigzagged constantly over the humpy ground in frantic efforts to shake off their pursuers; but the dogs always checkmated their efforts to reach the brush.

When at last the two packs merged, and Tawny turned right-about-face so abruptly that Golden Fur swept clear beyond him, she knew that they could do nothing but go back the way they had come. Ahead of them lay only the river, swollen now with heavy rains.

Then began the maddest chase that the spotted pair had ever known. For upwards of two hours, they swept across the open plain, running first toward the jungle and then away from it. Try as they might, they never found a chance to dart into the gloomy recesses of the forest. Their lungs were straining and their sides were heaving with each breath.

The race had tired the dogs and the hunters too. All except one man seemed to have left success or failure to the weary hounds that bounded along with their pink tongues hanging out. The owner of the rifle dashed out from time to time and *bang-bang*ed at the quarry.

As the shadows lengthened, Golden Fur dropped slowly back. When the panting Tawny glanced at Golden Fur's heaving sides, he slackened his pace;

then once more the two great cats ran on together.

On and on the jaguars circled. Behind them—then ahead of them—then behind them again lay the jungle that they could not reach.

All at once Tawny thought that Golden Fur was trying to tell him something. He remembered how she had been making little whimpering noises. Then he saw her stagger as she angled over the rough ground toward him.

It was as if she was telling him to leave her, telling him to run on alone! She was desperately tired. Her legs were giving out. Her head was whirling. Her heart was almost bursting. Without words she let him know that she had a plan for herself. She knew an easier death than to be tortured by men and dogs.

Without giving Tawny a chance to answer her, Golden Fur signaled him a last good-bye. Then she drew on a final ounce of strength and sped toward the river that lay only one thousand feet away.

Tawny did not even hear the cheers of the hunters and the rage of the dogs. He seemed hardly to realize that he was free now to speed forward as fast as he could. Nothing now held him back.

All he thought of was Golden Fur and her decision. *Which should he choose for himself? Death lay behind him! Death lay ahead!* Suddenly he chose to follow his mate.

Although he could hear the dirge of the river ahead of him, he turned to the right and raced toward the stream just as though he were going to victory.

Golden Fur outdistanced him. With never a backward glance, she neared the stream. At its brink, she hurtled through the air and sailed far out over the swollen river.

At her disappearance Tawny the Magnificent did not hesitate for even a split second. Heedless of shouts and the roar of the water, the great male gathered himself for the leap. With a rumble that died in his golden throat, he hurled his great body out—out—into empty space.

It seemed a long, long time before he struck the water. When he hit, he sank like iron. Almost at the very second that he disappeared from sight, a bullet followed from the bank behind him. *Sput!* The water spattered at the spot where he had gone down.

The jaguar did not come to the surface quickly enough to see the hunting party crash wildly along the bank. He did not see the men leap from their panting animals and peer eagerly down to see whether the *jacarés* or the piranhas had already risen to find their prey. He did not hear the men asking each other excitedly, "Do you think the jaguars will come up?"

All at once a man yelled as he pointed toward the river excitedly. There was one golden head, then two. The jaguars were still alive, still safe! Their dripping heads glistened in the sunlight as the two great beasts bobbed about in the center of a current.

Golden Fur fought the current bravely. She seemed to be making headway toward the opposite shore, but Tawny was floundering. The watchers thought that he could not make the other bank that was fringed with heavy undergrowth. All at once he disappeared.

After what seemed an age, he reappeared. Then he sank again. Even before the jaguar could have time to rise, the hunter with the rifle calculated the distance coolly. Drawing back and dropping to one knee, he cocked the hammer of his gun.

When Tawny finally rose, gulping and gasping for breath, the marksman slowly lowered his gun. This time the weapon might have fired perfectly. This time his aim might have been perfect; however, something about the jaguar's gallant efforts aroused the hunter's admiration and kept him from firing.

In silence the men stood watching the swimmers. Very cautiously Golden Fur dodged uprooted trees. Very skillfully she twisted herself around forest debris.

When she was more than two-thirds across the stream, she slackened her pace until the almost winded Tawny overtook her. Then very slowly the jaguars breasted the torrent side by side.

Tawny emerged first from the river to stand upon the farther shore. Gently he nuzzled Golden Fur as she crawled out beside him.

Suddenly the great male pushed his muzzle upward. Then he blasted the silence with a roar of victory. As the sound echoed across the Tapajos River and over the jungle grassland, it announced that Tawny had won over his enemies.

As if to show his contempt for man, dog, and river, the great male blared out another ear-splitting roar. Then before its echo had died away, the king of Brazilian jaguars turned his back upon his foes.

With a signal for Golden Fur to follow him, the great beast led the way into an unfamiliar jungle. Tawny of the Mato Grosso was still alive, still free, still undefeated!

* * * * *

"Tawny," by Edith Bowden. Published in The Boys' World, *January 10, 1937. Printed by permission of Joe Wheeler (P.O. Box 1246, Conifer, CO 80433) and David C. Cook, Colorado Springs, CO 80918. Edith Bowden wrote for mid-twentieth-century magazines.*

The Elephant That Cried

Eric B. Hare

Out of the interstices of my childhood, every once in a while an image floats upward into my conscious thoughts: a mesmerizing missionary storyteller from what was then called Burma (now Myanmar). We kids were enthralled whenever we heard him telling stories, first by Eric B. Hare's incredibly expressive voice (once heard, impossible to confuse it with anyone else's), but then by his rubbery face, which he could contort at will, and eyebrows that constantly twitched. This is the reason why print is unable to fully recapture the experience of hearing/seeing him alive.

This particular story is just one of the many he told—the Burmese called their beloved doctor "Dr. Rabbit." His associate, Harold Baird, became known as "Dr. Bear."

* * * * *

One morning one of the school boys rushed into my office. "Dr. Rabbit! Dr. Rabbit!" he cried breathlessly. "Dr. Bear wants you at the dispensary quick! He says to tell you it's a big lady patient. She's so big he can't get her through the front double door of the dispensary. Please hurry!"

I was instantly on my way. *Whatever could it be?* I thought to myself as I

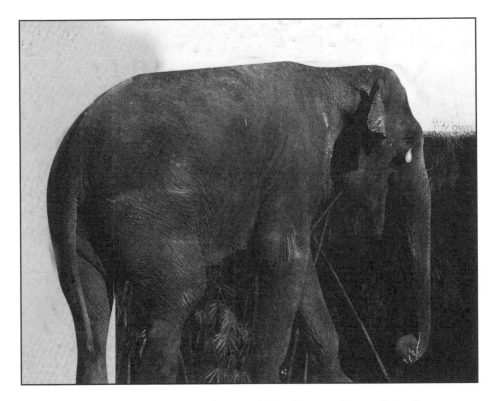

raced along. But very soon I understood, for there in front of the dispensary, with six jungle workmen standing around her, stood a huge female elephant! "Dr. Bear!" I said. "What can I do to help you with your big lady patient?"

"Look there!" he directed, pointing to her hip. "She was gored by a male elephant's tusk, and now the wound is infected."

I looked and saw a huge swelling as big as a five-gallon can. The poor elephant was in agony. She stamped her foot restlessly and tried to reach the sore place with her trunk.

"Tell the men to have the elephant lie down." Dr. Bear got into action. "We've got to make that hole big enough to get the hose in so we can wash it out with some carbolic solution," he explained.

It took a little time to cut a bigger hole in the elephant's hide—it was an inch thick. Then I worked the pump while he directed the flow of the solution to all parts of the swelling. To finish up he packed in several yards of gauze and said to the thankful owner, "Come again tomorrow."

He did come again the next morning, and marvel of marvels, it took only one command from the owner, and the huge patient lay down for her treatment.

"She's much better," said the owner. "She's not so nervous anymore."

Dr. Bear gave the wound another good hosing out and said, "Come again tomorrow."

While we were at breakfast the next morning the elephant's owner came running up the stairs into the house. "Have you seen my elephant?" he cried. "We gave her her food last night at our camp three miles away. And this morning we can't find her anywhere."

"Surely no one would steal a sick elephant!" I said. "Did you look over at the dispensary?"

He ran off to look, and in a minute he was back with a big grin on his face. "She's there, all right," he said, "lying under the tree waiting for her treatment!"

You may have read that elephants have remarkable memories and are very intelligent. Take it from me, this is true. For six weeks after that, Mrs. Elephant came *by herself* to the dispensary every morning and lay down by herself, waiting for her treatment.

When the six weeks were up and the wound was healed, the owner mounted her head and said to her, "We're going away now. Say '*salaam*' to the doctors." The big lady patient kneeled down and saluted us with her trunk. I thought she deserved a going-away present, so I gave her a small loaf of bread. As she took it with her trunk and put it in her mouth (I know you won't believe this, but it's true!), tears ran out of her eyes and flowed down her cheeks! I think Dr. Bear had tears in his eyes too. I didn't look. I was too busy blowing my own nose.

* * * * *

"The Elephant That Cried," by Eric B. Hare. Published by permission of Patti Hare Swensen, Pacific Press® Publishing Association, and Review and Herald® Publishing Association. Eric B. Hare, famed missionary doctor to Burma, was well known for his stories and public reading performances during the first half of the twentieth century.

THE ARMS OF AHMED

Julia K. Hildreth

This story took place back in the days when Great Britain ruled India. It was a quiet day when Ahmed tiptoed in to see how Baby Percy was doing. As soon as the master returned from his hunt, it would be back to work. Now would be a good time to play on his beloved piccolo.

Raising it to his mouth—he froze . . .

* * * * *

How cool and fresh it was after the glaring heat of the Indian day! The many doors and windows of the bungalow were thrown open to admit the sweetly scented breeze. The white curtains waved softly backward and forward under the deep-roofed veranda. From one of the apartments came a low, crooning sound: Golab, the *ayah,* or nurse, was singing the little one to sleep.

Ahmed, as he glided by, caught a glimpse of the lace-trimmed cradle, and dear little Percy's great blue eyes watching him.

Every one upon the plantation loved Baby Percy, or "Percy Baba," as the natives called him. He was not peaked and cross like most English children living in India, but smiling and rosy as the sky at dawn. But no one, not even the *"Mem Sahib"* herself, loved little Percy as did Ahmed. He worshiped the very ground upon which the child's tiny feet rested.

But Nurse Golab was a jealous old woman and would scarcely allow Ahmed to look at her charge. He saw her white-robed figure crouching by the cradle now, and paused, half resolved to run in and touch his lips to the dimpled hand as it lay on the silken coverlet.

The child's bed stood midway in the long room, or, rather, hall; the door at each end was opened wide. From where he stood, Ahmed could see through the opposite doorway; in the distance, a tiny temple, a blue lake, and part of a dark bamboo thicket.

Before the boy could quite make up his mind to brave the *ayah*'s anger, she looked up and warningly raised her dusky finger. So he went on, his bare feet making no sound on the veranda floor.

Next he reached a small apartment with a hammock swung in one corner under a shelf decorated with rifles, pistols, a pair of foils, and a cartridge belt. But none of these possessed the smallest attraction for Ahmed. He was searching for something he had that morning spied through the window.

"It is mine," he muttered, as his hand touched the smooth surface of his little fife, a piccolo. "Old Golab had no right to take it from me."

He thrust the small musical instrument under his gown and darted away, fleet-footed as an antelope. Around the corner of the bungalow he hurried; through the garden, past the lotus-covered fountain with an empty water jar upturned beside it; then, vaulting over a low brick wall, he sped along the rough cart road leading to the mango grove. As he came in sight of the ruined temple, he hesitated, for he thought he detected a movement in the dense shadow at the base. It might be the *Burra Sahib*—the master—and the hunters coming home. That morning they had left the plantation, armed to the teeth, and had gone into the thicket after the great man eater which had been seen prowling around—the same beast, it was thought, that had seized a child of one of the natives as it lay asleep in the shade near a hut.

Ahmed knew that if the master returned, he would be wanted at once; so, seating himself on a fallen tree, he watched the spot.

As he did so he passed his hand over the polished surface of the piccolo.

"Yes, it is mine," he muttered again. "No one has a right to take it from me, for my *Chota Sahib* gave it to me when he went away."

Then Ahmed musingly recalled how kind this young Englishman had been

to him, and how much pains he had taken to teach him to bring music from the little flute in his hand.

Everyone else living on the plantation disliked the sound of its high, shrill tones. Even the dogs howled in chorus if he so much as placed it to his lips. So he and his *Chota Sahib,* as Ahmed called the young Englishman, used to retire to this very mango grove and practice together by the hour.

And Ahmed thought no sound could quite equal the beauty of the piccolo's clear notes. One day at lunch (called *tiffin* in India), while he waited at table, a gentleman told a story of how the effect of various musical sounds had been tried upon the animals in the Zoological Gardens in London. He said that while the tones of the violin had been received with signs of pleasure by the four-footed audience, the piccolo was universally detested, even the majestic lion and the fierce Bengal tiger being cowed and terrified by its piercing notes.

This story had grieved Ahmed. He was somewhat comforted, however, when his friend and teacher had explained to him that the animals' dislike and fear of the instrument was no doubt caused by the effect of the high and rapid vibrations of sound produced by it on their extremely sensitive organs of hearing.

After the young Englishman left India, Ahmed had ventured to try a few notes on his beloved piccolo to amuse his darling Percy; but Golab had snatched it from his hand and hid it. That was two weeks before; and though he had since searched for it everywhere, it was only this morning that Ahmed had discovered its whereabouts. And now that it was once more in his possession, he determined to retain it thereafter.

Ahmed held the piccolo to his lips and tried all its stops softly, as he watched the distant bamboo thicket looming up against the level skyline.

Nothing was stirring there now, and Ahmed had just time to decide that it was safe to proceed, when—something stole across the cart road before him, and with a stealthy movement slunk into a field of sugarcane standing between him and his master's dwelling.

The boy's breath came and went in gasps; for though the glimpse was but momentary, he had recognized the tawny, dark-striped coat of the dreaded tiger, the fearful man eater.

To save himself was Ahmed's first thought; but instantly he remembered the bungalow, with not a man about to protect the women and the children; and then suddenly the boy thought of dear, innocent, helpless little Percy lying in his cradle, a tempting morsel for the savage beast.

If Ahmed could only reach the house before the arrival of the crawling creature—in time to close the doors—the tiger might not enter, and the baby might be saved!

With trembling limbs and chattering teeth, Ahmed skirted the tall, golden stalks of sugarcane, and with a step almost as noiseless as the tiger's own, reached the brick wall of the garden. As he prepared to mount it, he saw that the tiger was there before him. It stood by the basin of the fountain upon which the great lotus blossoms rested, greedily lapping the water. As Ahmed's hand touched the wall, the animal drew in its breath and flattened its fur, as though to reduce its size as far as possible, and crouching to the earth, slunk beneath the heavy foliage.

Instead of scaling the wall, the boy bent low and hurried on until he reached a small iron gate opening into the garden. Nothing obstructed his view of the bungalow, for the flowering shrubs and shade trees all were on the other side. So he ran on toward the hall where only a few moments ago he had seen little Percy.

On the threshold he stumbled over the prostrate form of Golab, the *ayah*. She lay face downward, too frightened to move.

His eyes took in the interior of the room at one glance, and ever afterward the scene remained indelibly impressed upon his memory: the white cradle, the rosy occupant kneeling among the pillows, his hands resting on the rail, and his face, which wore a half-pleased, half-curious expression, turned expectantly toward the opposite door. The open portal framed the evening sky, glowing and golden; and low down on the veranda floor crouched the dark form of the tiger, motionless save for the waving of its tail.

Ahmed was afraid, and he knew he was afraid; but the sight of his idol's danger banished every thought of self, and with that disdain of life which in supreme moments marks the Indian native, he stepped over the body of Golab and planted himself between the baby and the savage beast.

The tiger raised its head, and its eyes glittered with rage; then with lowered head it again seemed to measure the distance that lay between itself and the boy.

He will strike me from his path and seize my precious one! thought Ahmed, in horror.

There was no means of defense within reach, and Ahmed dared not stir one inch from his place. He clutched firmly the slender piccolo, which he still retained in his hand. As he grasped this ineffectual weapon, and the animal crawled a few inches nearer, he felt the stops of the instrument press against his palm. Then suddenly the conversation he had listened to some weeks ago came into his mind.

Perhaps it was true, thought Ahmed, *and at the worst I can but die!*

Then he whispered, "Lie still, Percy Baba!" and with a swift movement, raised the piccolo to his lips.

The first wild notes which came from the instrument were like the shriek of agony. The crouching tiger started erect. Uttering a cry of rage at the next sound, it shook its great head, and the bristling hairs on the sides of its face stood out like brushes. Then it moved backward a step, as if astonished and terrified.

Noting this retreat, Ahmed stepped cautiously forward. Involuntarily his lips and fingers formed the notes of a wild native air. As he glided forward, the great man-eating tiger drew ever backward; and so, with his dark eyes fixed on the big glistening orbs of the beast, Ahmed bravely followed, while the piccolo ever wailed and screamed forth the mournful music.

On went the strange pair, neither turning to the right nor left, or removing his gaze from the other's eyes; down the gravel walk, out through the gate, along the edge of the waving sugarcane, over the rough cart-road—Ahmed advancing and timing his steps to the slow, backward crawling of the fascinated brute.

They had reached the fallen tree, and the mango grove was just beyond.

Now Ahmed's breath came in gasps; his lips were glued to the piccolo, they were so dry. He felt that in a few seconds he must pause, and he knew right well that at that moment the tiger would spring upon him.

But I have saved the little one—I have saved Percy Baba! he thought, as he made a last and ineffectual attempt to draw forth another note.

Ahmed's hands fell to his sides, and he stood waiting, numb and cold with fear of the coming attack.

The tiger paused in its backward crawl, crouched low, and crept toward the boy again, with quivering haunches, blazing eyes, and bristling hair. Already its hind legs were braced for the spring, when—*Ping! Ping! Ping!*—three tiny spurts of flame darted from the bushes behind, and the tiger rolled over on its back, limp and lifeless.

The next moment Ahmed was surrounded by the three skillful hunters who had that morning gone in search of the dreaded monster now lying harmless at the feet of the fainting boy.

One of the hunters carried Ahmed home to the bungalow, taking the boy on his back, for Ahmed was for some little time too unstrung to walk.

It was Golab, the *ayah,* who, seated upon the floor weeping and wringing her hands in excitement, told the whole story: how she had been singing the baby to rest, and, glancing up, was horrified to see a pair of blazing eyes watching her; how she knew no more until the piccolo aroused her. Then she described minutely all that followed the coming of Ahmed.

From that day Ahmed was a privileged character. His piccolo might have been played in every corner of the place. No one—least of all old Golab—ever thought of denying him anything. The poor woman could never do half enough to repay the boy for rescuing her dear little charge from the dreadful man-eating tiger, whose skin now lay under Ahmed's hammock, and whose teeth, strung upon a golden cord, ornamented his breast as a trophy justly won by his courage and presence of mind.

* * * * *

"The Arms of Ahmed," by Julia K. Hildreth. Published in St. Nicholas, May *1900. Original text owned by Joe Wheeler. Julia K. Hildreth wrote for popular magazines during the first half of the twentieth century.*

CONDOR EGGS

Albert W. Tolman

It seemed so easy: all he had to do was climb up through the rocks to the condor nest. True enough, he made it.

But what he hadn't counted on was the speed at which condors could plunge from the sky. The parent birds now fought a desperate fight for the safety of their chicks.

Who would win out?

* * * * *

Frelon Marsh shot a startled glance behind him at Dorothy Amsden's cry of alarm. The four, Juan ahead, then Frelon, Dorothy, and her brother Roy, were trudging with their stout iron-pointed sticks along the ancient disused Andes trail. Down this, fabled millions in bullion had been transported on llamas from the lost Inca gold mine. The rough slippery path was barely three feet wide. On the left, high cliffs rose; on the right yawned a canyon two thousand feet deep. Juan, the Indian guide, carried a hundred-foot coil of small stout rope, looped over his shoulders; the others had only light knapsacks of food.

"What's the matter?" demanded Frelon of the English girl.

"Roy! He's disappeared!" She stood still, her face white. Juan and Frelon halted. The two had just rounded a sharp corner. Roy was nowhere to be seen.

"Don't worry!" comforted Frelon. "I'll look him up. He can't be far."

Edging carefully past her, he stepped back round the projecting bluff. The trail along which the four had just come was visible for over a quarter-mile, and Roy was not on it.

Frelon had spoken with Roy not a half-minute before; now he was gone. Worse still, his staff and knapsack lay close to the bluff. Could the English boy have fallen into the canyon?

Dorothy joined him. As the two stared in silence along the trail, a slight scratching overhead drew their attention upward. Thirty feet above them was the missing Roy, clambering up the almost perpendicular cliff.

Relief mingled with fresh alarm in Dorothy's cry. "Where in the world are you going?"

Her brother paid no attention to her appeal. "I want to take a look at that condor's nest Juan pointed out to us the other day."

"You never can get up there!" cried Dorothy.

"Pooh! This is nothing. I've climbed lots of harder places in the Alps." Roy kept on climbing.

Horace Marsh, Frelon's father, was the American manager of the Francisco copper mine in the Peruvian Andes. Frelon, seventeen, just through high school in the states, was spending a year with his parents in South America before beginning his course in mining. Strong, active, and deeply interested in his future work, he had not only gone through the Francisco from top to bottom, but in addition had done a lot of exploring in the nearby mountains, accompanied by a Spanish Indian named Juan. Frelon's imagination had been fired by the tradition that in the vicinity lay an old Inca gold mine, the exact location of which had been lost for almost four hundred years. Even though he had little hope of finding this mine, hunting for it was an exciting game.

Bruce Amsden, an English stockholder, had come to inspect the Francisco; with him were his wife, his son, and his daughter. While Mrs. Marsh and Mrs. Amsden were enjoying each other's company and their husbands were at the mine, the young people, accompanied by Juan, organized an eager search for the lost bonanza.

The English boy, feeling himself an experienced globe-trotter, was a little inclined to patronize the American. Frelon did not relish this, but he thought Roy a good fellow and enjoyed his company.

Mrs. Amsden had talked privately with Frelon about her son. "Keep an eye on Roy, won't you? Don't let him do anything too risky. He takes chances, and now and then he gets into a bad scrape." Frelon promised. He was glad to oblige Mrs. Amsden.

One afternoon the three young people had been out with Juan on an unfrequented trail high among the barren mountains. As they passed under a projecting crag, the Indian had pointed upward. "A condor's nest!"

Over the edge of a shelf about fifty feet high protruded a bird's head at the end of a long bare neck. At Juan's words Roy was all attention. "I'd like to see one of the eggs!"

Frelon laughed. "You'll never do that!"

"Why not?"

"Condors are unpleasant birds to bother."

Roy had said nothing more but evidently did not forget. A week later on the same trail, he dropped behind and started climbing.

Despite all remonstrances, he kept on toward the shelf. There were no signs of any condors. Roy was a good mountaineer and used every finger and toe to the best advantage. The three below held their breath as he wriggled over the last projection and gained the ledge. He stood up, looked, and shouted out, "Two eggs!"

Juan was uneasy. "Better come down. The birds may come back any minute!"

Roy looked at the sky above the black jagged peaks. "Not a thing in sight! Besides, I'm not afraid of 'em."

"You do not know condors. They can see for miles, and they fly like the wind. They are a match for a full-grown man."

Suddenly the Indian, who had been gazing apprehensively at the west, uttered a cry of alarm. "See! See! They are coming!"

Frelon and Dorothy, looking anxiously, saw two black specks, rapidly growing larger. Frelon shouted a warning. "The birds'll be here in a minute! Come down quick!"

"Just as soon as I get those eggs!" called Roy.

A few steps brought him to the nest. As he bent over it, Juan gave a hoarse yell that Frelon echoed.

"Roy! Oh, Roy! Look out!" shouted Dorothy.

With harsh, angry cries the furious birds were upon the boy. The three on the trail fifty feet below could only stand still and look helplessly up.

The condors were a terrifying sight, with long pointed wings spreading almost a dozen feet, bare necks, and white ruffs of down near their black-feathered bodies. They assailed Roy savagely with their arched beaks and strong curved claws.

Roy staggered back from the nest. He tried to beat his foes off with his arms, striving to protect his face and eyes. Pulling out his pocketknife, he stabbed at them, pluckily but uselessly.

Roy needed help now, if he ever did. Frelon remembered his promise to Mrs. Amsden, but what could he do?

Suddenly the boy flung himself backward and disappeared from sight. Where had he gone? The birds still swooped and darted in the place where he had stood. Frelon heard a muffled cry and shouted, "Roy! Roy! Where are you?"

"In a hole in the rock behind the nest!"

"Can't you get down?"

"How can I? The birds won't let me. Help me somehow! Drive 'em off! They're tearing at my feet and legs!"

Dorothy grasped Frelon's arms. "Can't you do something?"

Roy's yells of pain grew louder. "This hole's too small for me to get in out of their reach!"

Frelon understood the situation perfectly. Roy's only line of retreat lay toward the nest, but the instant he started that way, the condors would think he was after their eggs and would fight him back. Even if he could reach the edge of the shelf, he would surely be beaten off.

Frelon's many tramps through the mountains had made him resourceful. As his eyes searched the steep bluff, an idea came to him. "Let me take your rope," he said to Juan. "Dorothy, lend me your sweater."

Frelon tied its sleeves around his neck and hung the rope at his side. He thrust his stick under his left arm and through his belt, so as to leave both hands free. He began climbing the bluff.

The stick hampered him badly, yet he dared not cast it away. Without some kind of a weapon, he could not hope to battle successfully with the furious birds. Muffled shouts, mingled with the sound of swooping wings and hoarse screams, told him that the condors were keeping Roy busy. Frelon climbed faster.

At last he reached the shelf. Ten yards away Frelon could see the two white eggs. Nearby, the birds were darting at Roy's feet. Roy had crawled as far as he could into a crevice and was kicking vigorously at his foes. Blood was running from his legs.

"I'm coming!" called Frelon. He heard a glad cry. He glanced along the ledge but saw no place to fasten the rope. Disappointed, he looked up. Above rose a sharp point of rock. That would do, if he could get up there. He began climbing again.

Soon Frelon reached the upper ledge. As his head came level with it, he noticed something that for an instant almost made him forget Roy. A yell startled him. "Hurry! I can't stand this much longer!"

Making a slip noose of the rope end, Frelon looped it over a nodule of rock, then dropped the rope down the face of the cliff. The rope crossed the shelf of the condors and almost reached the trail. Letting the closely twisted strands slip through his fingers, he slid down a short distance until he stood on the narrow platform near the nest.

Roy was shouting and kicking aimlessly at the swooping birds. "Be ready, Roy! Do as I tell you! Come out, and slide down this rope! Don't wait!"

Scrambling hastily out of the crevice, Roy caught the rope and swung himself down it toward the trail. The fury of the birds was now turned on Frelon.

He had all he could do to defend himself. Back set against the rock, he wielded his stick, desperately beating off his foes. At last a shout came from below. "I'm down!"

Roy was safe. Frelon retreated along the ledge toward the dangling rope. As the condors circled away after a vicious assault, he pushed the stick through his belt and wrapped his head in Dorothy's sweater. Grasping the rope with both hands, he swung off the shelf and began sliding down.

Perhaps the birds would let Frelon alone now. No! In they darted again, stabbing, clawing, rending his unprotected arms and body. How long could he endure such torment?

Down he slid, fast, but not too fast, blinded by the muffling folds of the sweater. Suddenly the attacks ceased. Hands caught Frelon's legs and body. A moment later his feet struck the trail.

Frelon unwrapped his head and gave the sweater back to Dorothy. "If it hadn't been for that, those birds would have pecked my eyes out. I'm sorry it's torn."

"What you've done for Roy is worth a thousand sweaters!"

"You saved my life," declared Roy.

Frelon felt embarrassed. "Let's get back to the mine. I've a surprise for my father."

As the four started to return, the condors, left masters of the battlefield, circled triumphantly overhead.

Two hours later the party reached the Francisco.

Roy cherished a rankling grudge against the condors. "We'll go back and shoot 'em!"

"No," retorted his father. "Let the birds alone. They were defending their home. They had a right to drive you off."

Frelon broke in with startling news. "When I was on the upper ledge, I believe I found that old Inca gold mine."

An exploring party the next day discovered that he was right. It was the old mine and a rich one.

"Those condors must be related to the goose that laid the golden eggs," declared Horace Marsh. "We won't begin work on that mine until they've hatched out their young and gone. That would be playing fair."

* * * * *

"Condor Eggs," by Albert W. Tolman. Published in The Boys' World, *July 15, 1933. Printed by permission of Joe Wheeler (P.O. Box 1246, Conifer, CO 80433) and David C. Cook, Colorado Springs, CO 80918. Albert W. Tolman (1866–1965), educator and author, was a prolific writer of stories for popular magazines during the late nineteenth and early twentieth centuries.*

BROKEN!

Marjorie Grant Burns

It is not mere coincidence that one of the fastest automobiles of our time—the Cobra—is named after it, for the serpent's strike is faster than the human eye can follow or reflexes avert in time.

Many years ago it was when I first read this true story—it has haunted me ever since.

* * * * *

An odd, heavy stillness hung over the deep jungle paths as another hot day faded slowly, lingering on treetops and climbing the distant mountain peaks.

As the last rays departed, the daytime jungle life took to its resting place, and night prowlers came stalking out. In the dense grass a deadly cobra uncoiled and slithered along, silent and unseen. Somewhere in that darkening jungle the beginning of a strange destiny awaited this deadly reptile.

Thousands of miles away an attractive woman in her early thirties hurried across her garden and into her sunny kitchen. Pushing back her hair and smiling a little to herself, she brought out some vases and cut and arranged her load of flowers. That she would be involved in the destiny that

was beginning in the jungle so far away never entered her mind. She took up one vase, paused a moment at the distant tolling of a church bell, then pushed the door shut against the early fall chill.

Into this strange web on this same day another was drawn as surely as time moves its stealthy way. Picking up a new and shiny card, he regarded it in the mirror. It read backward, but how well he knew what it said: "Press Photographer." He had dreamed and planned for this a long time; now he was definitely on his way. Could he have seen what lay behind those two words, he would have turned back. But he did not see; he could not know; time took him down a path of no returning.

* * * * *

Months later fog settled over a large metropolitan city in the western United States, and the dismal toot and wail of fog horns on the bay mingled with the traditional morning din. Weary drivers peered at endless creeping mazes of glaring lights, heads ached, and tempers were short. Traffic fought its way to work slowly.

Burt Hunter pulled in at press headquarters. Reaching over, he fingered down the lock buttons, picked up his equipment, put on his hat, got out, and locked the car door. A sharp tap on a window two stories up caught his attention. He gazed intently a moment, then nodded to indicate he would be up. Five minutes later he walked into the editor's office.

"Say, Burt, assignment here. Human interest. Short story and several pictures. Got your car this morning?"

"Yeah, but a lot of good it does in this pea-soup atmosphere!"

"It'll clear soon. This is suburb stuff out on Asherton Road. Reptile trainer."

"Reptile trainer! Take pictures of one of those mental wanderers. Who said?"

"The boss said. Besides, this one is a little less than crazy. Scientific and all that. Nationally known. She has lectured all over the country."

"What am I getting into? Does she try to get you to hold her little pets?"

"Not these little pets, pal. These are cobras, pure and simple. And she trains them. Now get going. Here's the address."

Taking the slip, Burt cast his friend a sarcastic look and stamped out.

Cobras indeed! What a goose chase. What is a newspaper business coming to when it sends out an expert photographer to photograph snakes? He made a face. What some people would not do to get into the news, but now this cobra gets there by mere virtue of its arriving. "Great life," he mutters. "Snake portraits, by Burt Hunter."

Anyway, it was clearing. Burt's spirits lifted as the clouds broke and the sunshine poured through.

"Oh, what a beautiful morning,
Oh, what a beautiful day,
I got a—"

His singing stopped abruptly as the descending address numbers singled out a spacious home set among the pines on the crest of a hill. It was a beautiful place, and he liked beautiful things. An enormous picture window suggested something worthwhile behind him—he turned to look, and the poet in him responded like a leap of flame. The hill dropped away suddenly; and there, far below, held static by the distance, lay the shimmering colors of brown and emerald, white, and then deeper green of the ocean, translucent in the early morning sun. A gentle wind tugged at pine boughs, and they made a soft soughing sound, as if sighing over the endless beauty below. He sighed with them and turned back up the path and to the door. Pressing the button, he was immediately announced by vibrant chimes. A moment later a smiling face appeared at the portal.

Burt Hunter's first reaction was that he surely had the wrong address. The evident beauty and taste and refinement surely did not mix with cobras. He stated his errand almost with apology.

"Oh, yes. You're at the right place. Come in, won't you? I guess I didn't appear quite like you expected, but you see—I don't do this just for fun. It's a scientific experiment. The cobras are safe as long as *I* handle them. I understand them. But I am always very careful. Their bite is deadly, you know."

"Yes, I certainly *do* know. I can't imagine such an attractive person as you appear to be choosing such a profession. It certainly isn't necessary, is it?"

"Well, no, not exactly. But there is a fascination about it. To test your wits against something so deadly—well, you'll just have to admit it is no small challenge. It does take something to do it."

"No doubt. But lots of other things are a challenge too—and more useful—and less dangerous. Why, if you keep on, something is bound to happen to you. You simply *can't* beat the law of averages."

"You sound as if you might care a little—if something did happen." Her smile was tinged with seriousness.

"Certainly I'd care. Frankly, you seem very nice to me, too nice to throw yourself away for a half-dozen cobras."

She studied his frank gaze a moment, and oddly moved, she turned to look out across the bay. No one had been concerned about her personal safety before. It was comforting, even from a complete stranger. She felt grateful to him. Turning back, she said, "Most folks just sort of jeer me on. You make me feel different about it somehow. But it isn't quite so serious as it seems. I can stop anytime; in fact, I plan to stop soon. Flowers are my second love. I have a beautiful garden, and I love to work in it."

She paused again, then suddenly remembering her guest's errand, she said, "Oh, but you wanted to take pictures. Suppose you set up over there, and I'll put the snakes here in the sunlight. Flash bulbs will upset them."

"Fine. But can you bring them in alone? I'll help—if I'm needed." He grinned.

"No, you must not come near them at all. The new one is a little hard to manage yet. We may have to leave him in his cage."

Burt Hunter was already setting up his cameras, but now he whirled around sharply.

"You mean—you take them out of their cages?"

"Certainly. Poor trainer I'd be if I couldn't do that. Look, Mr. Hunter, I don't fool in this business. I take no chances beyond bare necessity. You may feel a little unsure, but if you'll just do as I say, there is no danger." She smiled reassuringly as she left the room to get her "pets."

Burt took out his handkerchief and mopped his face. This situation, it seemed to him, was getting entirely out of hand. Glancing around the room as he waited, he marveled at the beautiful furniture and the radiant blue of the rich Oriental rugs. Once again he felt the sharp prick of contradictions. Flowers, beauty, grace, intelligence, a lovely home—and cobras. Her voice, strange and different now, sharp with intentness, broke his line of thought.

"Mr. Hunter, success from now on depends largely upon you. You *must* keep your place behind your cameras. *Do not make a single sudden move.* If you drop something, leave it for a moment, then pick it up *slowly.* If you must speak to me, do so quietly and slowly. Now, are we ready?"

He nodded, and strange little prickles crept up and down his spine. She carried in three baskets and set them in the sunlight upon the table. As she worked and talked quietly, sometimes to Burt, sometimes to the snakes, Burt as quietly snapped pictures. He marveled at her control and at her strength to lift them as she did. He felt that he could not bear even to touch one.

He bent now for the last pictures. Through his camera he watched the new cobra, as he was put upon the table and coiled slightly with head raised and swaying, responding to her quite insistent voice. Then—he saw her tense, her face became rigid, and her hands clenched. Her voice died away. Burt's hands gripped the rods of his tripod, and he felt the sweat stream down over his face and body—but he dared not move. Eternity seemed to have gripped him! Now she spoke.

"Something is wrong! Just stay where you are—I'll have to put him back—but don't move or speak." As she spoke she reached over slowly and closed and fastened the first two baskets. Then, very slowly, she lifted the new snake, moved it gently to its basket, put it in, removed her hands slowly—when suddenly it struck, burying its fangs in her wrist.

Burt Hunter, watching through his camera, felt shock hit him hard as he saw that deadly snake strike. He trembled and felt his senses reeling. If only he could move, or do something. Now she pulled her hand loose, slapped the lid of the basket down, and fastened it. She turned to Burt as he stepped quickly to her. Her left wrist she gripped tightly with her right hand.

"Listen," she said. "Go through this door, and at the top of the stairs on the shelf is the snake serum. Get it quickly!"

He leaped up the stairs, snatched up the box, and was before her again.

"Take out the syringe and fit the needle on . . . yes . . . so . . . now, press the needle through that little rubber cap on the top of that tiny vial and withdraw the serum by pulling back the plunger."

Burt struggled with the unfamiliar task. His big hands trembled, and his fear almost engulfed him. But he gritted his teeth and followed as she ordered. Gripping the vial, he tried to insert the needle, but he trembled so that he missed. Gripping it tighter, he missed again. He rested his arm against the table, and gripping both syringe and vial desperately, he steadied to try again, when his voice gasped in an agony of unbelief. In that big strong hand of his, somehow the vial had broken. The serum dripped through his cold fingers, stood a moment in beaded drops upon the rich thick rug, then slowly seeped into the rug, and disappeared. The breath drained out of Burt harshly; he raised his dazed eyes to meet hers.

What does a man say when he has just broken a life with his two bare hands and thrown it away? When you stand before someone who at the very instant faces eternity because of you—at such a moment what does one say? Have words ever been invented to say at such a time? I think not.

Burt's lips moved twice before a whisper finally made his despair heard. Three small words, so very small, but asking for so much.

"Madam—*forgive me!*"

And her answer, very low—"Yes, surely." She must have known. Her agony would be over shortly, but his would live on and on to embitter all the rest of his life.

After a few minutes the whine of the siren was heard, and an ambulance pulled up at the door. First aid, and a swift ride—but it was all too late. In a brightly lighted operating room, surrounded by doctors who tried to save her against the hopeless odds, she died a painful death, and Burt Hunter became a haunted man, driven day and night by bitter memory.

And somehow her death haunts *me*. Amazing surely that she played with deadly serpents—more amazing still that we—you and I—should dare to play with other dangerous things! She felt that she could manage where others had failed, and she planned to stop soon—*but it wasn't soon enough*!

* * * * *

"Broken!" by Marjorie Grant Burns. Published in The Youth's Instructor, *December 25, 1951. Printed by permission of Joe Wheeler (P.O. Box 1246, Conifer, CO 80433) and Review and Herald® Publishing Association. Marjorie Grant Burns wrote for mid-twentieth-century family magazines.*

The Boy Mahout

Clark Brockman

Boon was afraid of the great elephant, declaring that there was only one man who could control Poo Rapatanahan.
Softly, fourteen-year-old Sewai declared, "I can do it."
And so the battle began—make that two battles!

* * * * *

Nai Kow, the old and wrinkled headman of the Ban Rai elephant camp in north Siam, looked scornfully at the mahouts who squatted around him. "Is there not a man among you?" he sneered. "Is there not an elephant rider who will dare climb to the neck of the tusker? When I was young, there was not an animal I feared—mild-tempered or mean. But the days of real men are passed. You are all women!"

"Nai Kow is bold because his age protects him," growled Boon, the largest and roughest of the ten mahouts. "Poo Rapatanahan is in a bad humor. The only man who can ride him is Chan Dang, and he is ill. Any other man who tries it is a fool!"

"You chatter like a monkey," scoffed Nai Kow. "And like a monkey, you chatter loudest when you are afraid!"

The great muscles stood out on Boon's shoulders and arms as he clenched his fists angrily. His lips curled back from his teeth, which were blackened with betel nut. "Silence, Old Head," he growled. "You are too weak to insult a man who can fight."

"You are afraid," repeated Nai Kow. "But Poo Rapatanahan must be kept in condition. He must be taken down to the river for his bath, and he must be taken today. He has been hitched to that tree for three days. Already the hobbles and ropes are galling his skin. Even on his back and sides the skin is dry and hard. If he is kept there, he will not be fit for work when Chan Dang is well. If we have high water before he gets well, there will be a stack of logs at the Devil's Elbow as big as a mountain. Mr. Smith will come up here as mad as a cholera-breeding spirit. We will all be in trouble then!"

"We can take care of the logs without Poo Rapatanahan," said Boon.

"He is the only elephant strong enough to swim against the murderous whirlpools at Devil's Elbow," said Nai Kow. "But I suppose you think your long-legged bag of bones can break up a stack there. *Maa!*" The old man raised himself on his thin, knotted legs. "I am through talking. Is there no one who dares give the tusker his bath?"

"I'll do it," said a soft voice.

The men turned. Standing just back of Boon was Sewai, the fourteen-year-old son of Chan Dang. He was stocky but could not have weighed over ninety pounds. He wore nothing but a pair of short blue pants. On his handsome face was the ever-present smile which made his name so appropriate. *Sewai* means "happy." In his right hand was a long stalk of sugarcane, and in his left, a brick.

The men gazed at the boy as though they did not understand what he was saying, their eyes fixed on him with incredulous stares.

"Maa!" snorted Boon.

"Not you, my boy," said Nai Kow. "I was talking to the men."

"But I promised my father I would give Poo Rapatanahan a bath."

"Your father does not know what he is saying. The fever has made him delirious. It is a man's work. You are not yet a man."

"I am the son of Chan Dang," replied Sewai. "Today I give Poo Rapatanahan a bath."

"Poo Gin will eat you up! Just like this, *Bruup!*" Boon made a terrible face and shook his ugly head as he growled.

"His name is Poo Rapatanahan," said Sewai. It was difficult for him to control his anger. Boon had insulted the tusker. *Poo Rapatanahan* means "the father who eats like a gentleman." Boon had called him *Poo Gin*—"the father who feeds like a dog."

"Poo Gin will eat you up!" repeated Boon.

Quick as a flash, Sewai swung the stalk of sugarcane over his shoulder and hit Boon on the head. Before the men could realize what had happened, the boy was running as fast as his legs would carry him to the tree where the tusker was tied.

"Yot [Stop]!" shouted Nai Kow. *"Mai dai* [It can't be done]!"

"Come back, you little toad," barked Boon, jumping to his feet.

Sewai slowed down as he approached the tusker, lest his sudden appearance startle the elephant, and went forward slowly, holding the sugarcane so that Poo Rapatanahan could take it.

The elephant evidently recognized his rider's son, for he showed no displeasure at the boy's approach. Sewai was in the habit of bringing him sugarcane and often rode with his father on Poo Rapatanahan's broad head.

The elephant wrapped the end of his long trunk slowly around the stalk, lifted it over his head in the salute Sewai had taught him, brought it down to his mouth, broke it in two and ground it between his corrugated teeth.

Sewai stood beside him, his hands behind his back. His head barely reached to the neck of the nine-foot elephant, while his body was no bigger around than Poo Rapatanahan's foreleg. But he stood there unafraid, talking to the elephant exactly as he had always done.

"Oh Father Who Eats Like a Gentleman," he said, "my father sends you greetings. He is worried because you have not been bathed. As I came by the temple I dug this soft brick out of the floor. Is it not a fine one?" He held the brick for the elephant to inspect. "It will make your skin as soft as a monkey's ear. Now kneel down so I can climb to your neck."

Poo Rapatanahan had finished his sugarcane. He looked at Sewai sourly.

"Kneel down," repeated Sewai.

The big tusker swayed his head back and forth slowly.

"Kneel down!" shouted Sewai in the tone of voice his father used when Poo Rapatanahan did not obey instantly.

Still he did not kneel. Sewai ran to a nearby bush and broke off a switch. He hurried back and stood before the tremendous head with its dangerous tusks.

"Stop!" shouted Nai Kow. "If you touch him, he will kill you! Keep away from him."

Sewai shook the switch before the gleaming white tusks. "Offspring of generations of fathers and mothers of mangy, flea-bitten, long-tailed rats! Son of a mouse—brother of caterpillars and cousin of toad frogs, kneel!" He switched the elephant's tender trunk. "Kneel," he commanded.

The great beast curled his trunk between his tusks and pulled his head back between his shoulders as though he were afraid.

"Kneel down, pig!"

Slowly Poo Rapatanahan knelt. Fearlessly Sewai stepped upon his leg, caught the top of his big ear, and pulled himself up to the elephant's neck. As soon as he was securely seated, he gave the order to rise. Poo Rapatanahan rose, lifting Sewai ten feet in the air.

"Loose the hobbles and give me a hook," called Sewai.

The men had been watching him with bated breath.

"Boon, loose the hobbles," ordered Nai Kow. "The boy is doing the impossible. And you thought you were a man! Loose the hobbles, I say! Choo, give the boy your driving hook."

Sullenly Boon went forward. Sewai ordered the tusker to raise his trunk, to make sure that Boon would not be hurt while the hobbles were being untied. Ankus in hand, he waited until the hobbles were loosed, then shook his left foot under the elephant's ear and gave the command to go. Poo Rapatanahan swung easily down the narrow trail leading to the river.

As he neared the bank he quickened his pace. He was almost running when he entered the pool. He thrust his trunk below the surface, sucked up a gallon of water, and shot it above his head in a lofty spray. Then he trumpeted!

Sewai clung to his great neck. For an hour he let Poo Rapatanahan splash and spray himself and trumpet. Then he guided the tusker to shallow water and made him lie down. As the elephant turned slowly on his side, Sewai jumped up and stood on his shoulder. He slipped the ankus into the back of his short pants and began rubbing the elephant's thick skin with the brick he had brought from the temple. For another hour he scrubbed and scoured, Poo Rapatanahan lying with his whole head under the water and only the tip of his trunk sticking out for air. When Sewai had scoured every part of his hide until it was soft and smooth, he took him back to the tying tree. One of the men fastened the hobbles, and Sewai slipped to the ground.

The riders gathered around Sewai. They were proud of the boy and frankly admitted that he could do things with Poo Rapatanahan that they would not dare to do. Boon was different. He blustered up to Sewai and caught him by the neck. "I'm going to teach you something," he threatened. The other riders stopped him, but he went away muttering and promising to teach Sewai some manners.

The next afternoon the boy gave Poo Rapatanahan another bath. When the tusker had been hobbled, the mahouts asked Sewai if he would be willing to come early the next day and take Poo Rapatanahan into the jungle to forage, for because of his present ill temper, they'd been afraid to turn the elephant loose; consequently all his food had to be cut and brought into camp. It was laborious work and especially irksome after a hard day straightening the logs that had caught on the banks of the stream.

Sewai agreed eagerly and scoffed at the idea of payment. He was thrilled. He had always wanted to take the big tusker into the jungle.

The next morning he was at camp with the earliest of the mahouts. Climbing to the elephant's neck, he started down a jungle trail to a place where the choicest shoots grew. He crouched low over Poo Rapatanahan's head, lest the branches of the trees sweep him to the ground. Several times during the day he was almost brushed off, and it was only by catching hold of the elephant's ears with both hands that he was able to keep from being knocked to the ground.

But Sewai enjoyed the day. When Poo Rapatanahan was foraging in the open jungle, he would crawl upon the great broad back and lie down at full length. Troops of monkeys jumped about in the trees over his head, chattered, scolded, played, and fought. Brilliant green parakeets circled over him in hundreds. Now and then he saw a pair of ugly hornbills, and once he saw three deer grazing a short distance off in the jungle.

That evening Sewai went home tired but happy. He had had no trouble with Poo Rapatanahan. He believed that he could make him work. For a long time he lay awake, thinking of how pleasant it would be to sit on the broad neck and make the elephant straighten the logs in the stream. He would be the smallest mahout riding the largest tusker in the herd.

The next morning, instead of taking Poo Rapatanahan into the jungle, he went upstream in search of the other riders. He found them a mile above camp. When he arrived, the men were sitting upon their elephants, jeering, and so intent on what was happening that they did not notice Sewai.

"You said your elephant could do it," bantered one of the men. "Tell him to push."

"His legs are too long," called another. "Cut them off a bit. He can't get down to the log."

Sewai saw Boon in the center of the group. His elephant was kneeling on the ground, with its head against a five-ton log. Boon was beating the animal with his ankus, shouting, cursing. The elephant was panting from its exertions and making no attempt to push. Boon had tired the beast and gained nothing.

"Baa!" shouted one of the riders. "Here is the Father Who Eats Like a Gentleman. Sewai, show Boon how to push the log."

Sewai hesitated. "I don't know how it should be done," he said. "I might make him waste his strength."

"He knows how to do it," replied Choo.

"He can't push any more than my elephant," growled Boon.

The riders shouted, "Show him!"

Sewai remembered that his father had said that Poo Rapatanahan had more sense than most men. So he guided the tusker to the end of the log, told him to kneel, and then gave the order to push.

Instead of pushing, Poo Rapatanahan got up, walked around to the opposite side of the log, and butted it with his broad forehead. The log moved. He hit it again and again, with short, hard strokes which made the log shake from end to end. At last it seemed to satisfy him. He walked around the log again, knelt down, placed his forehead against it, and pushed. The log moved as though it were no weight at all!

The riders shouted.

Boon said nothing, but riding close behind Poo Rapatanahan, he hit the elephant with his ankus. It was so unexpected and so hard that Poo Rapatanahan bellowed and went charging into the jungle, the branches of the trees and the trailing vines crashing before him.

Sewai was powerless to stop him. With the branches whipping over the elephant's back, it was all he could do to hang on. His ankus was jerked from his hand.

Poo Rapatanahan chose the densest part of the jungle for his mad charge. Branches pounded on Sewai's head and back. He crouched as close to the big neck as he could, holding on with his legs and gripping the big ears with his hands. He was tempted to let go. His shirt had been torn completely from his back, and each passing branch left a deep red scratch. He could catch one of those branches and swing to the ground, but that would be turning Poo Rapatanahan free.

Sewai knew that the first law for all mahouts is "Stick with your elephant." He realized that the tusker, in his present condition, would revert to the wild the moment he was free, and before he could be caught and held, might cause damage amounting to thousands of *ticals,* all of which the company would have to pay. But he knew, also, that as long as there was someone on Poo Rapatanahan's neck, the beast would remain a domesticated elephant.

Sewai determined to stick. When the tusker finally slowed down, the boy was scratched from head to foot. He was sore, he was bleeding, and he had lost most of his clothes. But he had stuck to his elephant.

Poo Rapatanahan trembled as he stood listening, waving his trunk to catch the scent of the enemy that had attacked him. After a long time he started foraging, but from time to time he would raise his trunk and feel the wind.

Sewai's whole body smarted and burned from the scratches. Myriads of gnats, mosquitoes, and even horseflies swarmed around him. He slapped and fanned continually but could not keep them away. He tried to get Poo Rapatanahan to return to camp, but without the driving hook, he was helpless.

It was an hour later that Choo found them. His face showed a mixture of surprise and pride. "I did not expect to find you on his neck," he said. "Many of the best mahouts could not have kept their seats in a charge like that. You have done well, Sewai." He handed the boy his ankus. "Take him home," he said.

Sewai applied the hook vigorously, and Poo Rapatanahan started back to camp at a brisk shuffle. When the elephant had been tied, Choo helped Sewai to the ground.

"Go and bathe," said the man.

Sewai moved stiffly to the stream and plunged in. The cool water soothed his burning skin, and when he finished bathing, Choo was waiting on the bank to grease his scratches. The rider carefully rubbed him from head to foot. He did not say a word until he had completed his task. Then he patted Sewai on the shoulder.

"Go home and rest," he said. "We are all proud of you. The other riders will attend to Boon as soon as the elephants are tied up tonight. He will never trouble you again."

But Choo's promise was not fulfilled. Even as he spoke, clouds were gathering in the east, and before the riders returned to camp it had started to rain. Nai Kow posted the men along the banks.

In the teak jungles, rain means work—hard, dangerous work. The logs that have been placed in the dry streams have to be watched when the rising water floats them. They have to be kept in the channel. Once a stack forms, it is difficult and dangerous to break it up, and the longer it stands the larger it gets. Every log above it is blocked. The men have to work as long as the water is high, riding their elephants into the raging current, dodging great logs that could crush both men and beasts.

The storm hit the top of the ridge first. What had been dry streams in the afternoon became raging torrents in a few minutes. High water reached the elephant camp almost as soon as the storm. The clear blue pool in which Sewai had bathed became a turbulent race of muddy water, with patches of dirty foam floating rapidly across it. Great five-ton logs splashed into the upper end, slid silently past the banks, and were caught again in the wild rush.

Up the valley could be heard the *boom! boom! bang!* made by the logs as they pounded into each other. At a distance it sounded like thunder, but as the logs moved closer to camp, it sounded like explosions of dynamite.

Boon had been stationed at Poo Rapatanahan's post, the short bend in the stream known as the Devil's Elbow. There the logs pounded into the great rock at the sharp turn with a boom that could be heard for miles. Boon was sullen and angry. He knew that it was probably the last time he would be working for the company and that the other riders would be waiting for him as soon as the flood was over. He took little or no interest in the work and would have done nothing except for the fact that Nai Kow kept a constant watch on him.

It was dangerous work. Where the stream turned, the water had dug a deep pool, where the muddy water whirled and boiled. No man could keep afloat in it at high water, and even the smaller elephants dared not enter.

As darkness settled down, bamboo torches filled with pitch were handed to the men. The lights sputtered and flared, casting fantastic shadows on the moving logs.

Nai Kow was called to another part of the stream to direct the breaking up of a stack. The moment he left, Boon guided his elephant up the steep bank and rested. He paid no attention to the booming of the logs in the pool below him. He paid no attention to the shouts of the rider on the opposite bank, warning him that a log had been caught. He sat sullenly shielding a palm-leaf cigarette from the drenching rain. When Nai Kow returned, a hundred logs had become wedged and packed into the narrow bend.

"Get down there and break up that stack," shrieked the old man, above the thundering of the logs.

Boon eyed the headman scornfully but did not answer.

"There are ten thousand logs up the stream," shouted Nai Kow. "If they pile up here it will take six months, possibly a year, to untangle them. Get down and break up that stack!"

"The stack is already too big," replied Boon. "But even if I could break it up I would not do it. There would be such a rush of water and logs that I would be crushed to death."

"The other elephants are not strong enough. You must go."

"I will not," replied Boon evenly.

Nai Kow was almost beside himself with anger. He was responsible for getting the logs to the river. He ordered Boon off the elephant and himself scrambled to the animal's neck. Although he had been a good mahout in his day, he had not ridden an elephant in years. But he was the headman, and he was responsible.

He took the elephant below the bend, swam the stream, and came up on the other side, where the water was not so deep and swift. Holding his torch high above his head as the elephant swam, he looked for the key log. At last he found it. It was almost submerged beneath the foaming water and wedged in with tons of logs and impounded water. His elephant could not move it.

He shouted to one of the men on the bank. "Get Sewai and Poo Rapatanahan. Hurry!"

The man darted into the jungle, but it was fully half an hour before he returned with Sewai and the Father That Eats Like a Gentleman. The stack was growing larger. Every few seconds a floating log would pound into it.

The old headman went close to Sewai and shouted, "Poo Rapatanahan is our only hope. No other elephant can move it now. Will you ride him in? It is dangerous. You may be carried down with the logs, although I believe Poo Rapatanahan will take care of you. He and your father broke up a stack here two years ago. Will you do it?"

"I will do it," replied Sewai.

"Good. Swim up below the stack. I will show you the key log. Just let Poo Rapatanahan do the work."

As his elephant went into the stream the cold, muddy water swirled around Sewai's waist. They neared the stack, and Sewai saw Nai Kow climbing over the jumbled logs, with a torch held high above his head. Behind him was Boon. The old man clambered down to the level of the water and put his foot on a log that was now completely covered.

"That's it," he shouted. "Poo Rap, that is the one. Pull it this way, toward the low water over there. The moment it lets go, get around that point. Move back quickly. Your life depends on it."

Already Poo Rapatanahan was feeling around the log with his trunk to find the *nepah* hole.

"Wait!" shouted Nai Kow. He handed the torch to Sewai and climbed quickly over the logs to the bank.

Boon stood on the top of the stack, still smoking. "I wish it would kill you both, but there is no such luck in the world. This stack will be here for months."

"Get off the stack," shouted Sewai.

Boon laughed.

"It is your last chance," cried Sewai. "I cannot wait!"

"Go on," sneered Boon.

Sewai looked at the threatening pile of logs. It did not seem possible that they could get out from under those logs, if they started down, but his father had done it. "Pull," he commanded.

The tusker's trunk tightened on the log as he threw his whole weight against it. It didn't budge.

Boom! Boom! The oncoming logs thundered into the upper end of the ever enlarging stack at the bend.

"Pull!" Sewai used his ankus. Poo Rapatanahan went through all the tricks he knew. He jerked, pulled, butted, twisted. The log turned a little.

The mad waters were swirling around the elephant's back and sides. The logs seemed to be stretching higher into the night. Boon still stood scornfully on the top.

"Twist it again," ordered the boy.

Poor Rapatanahan put his whole heart into it, lifting his huge bulk far out of the water. Just before he sank back into the water he shook it, as a terrier would shake a rat.

Above the thundering *boom! bang!* of the pounding logs rose a groan which ended in an ear-splitting wail. The logs were moving, and as they rubbed against each other they cried out like things human.

Sewai could see Boon on the top. His face, even in the flickering light, showed terror. He was shouting, but Sewai could hear nothing he said.

Already Poo Rapatanahan had started for the shallow eddy behind the sandbar opposite the giant rocks, swimming with incredible speed.

Sewai heard a roar. It seemed as though he were right in the midst of it. A wave washed him from his seat, but Poo Rapatanahan caught him and helped him back. They reached the calm of the eddy, and the tusker turned, as though he wanted to see the mad maelstrom he had created. The huge, blunt butts of upended logs passed within a few inches of Sewai's head, but none touched him. The elephant seemed to sense the dangerous ones before the boy could see them.

In the dim light cast by the torches, Sewai made out the figure of Boon. Somehow he had managed to keep alive, but the log on which he floated was being swept into the center of the maelstrom, where the grinding logs would crush him into a pulp.

"Forward!" ordered Sewai, kicking his feet beneath the tusker's ears. It was dangerous. One bump from those logs and they would be caught in the melee. Poo Rapatanahan moved closer to the writhing mass. He seemed to understand what was wanted of him, and he went forward quickly but cautiously, evading the logs as lithely as a water animal.

As they neared Boon, the elephant stretched out his trunk. Boon grabbed for it, but the tusker jerked it aside. He repeated the trick. The log which the man was riding would soon be out of reach. It seemed as though the elephant recognized in him the enemy who had struck him that morning. It was a horrible means of torture—safety was so close, yet unattainable. A dreadful death awaited!

Boon was almost out of reach when Poo Rapatanahan finally caught his outstretched hand and jerked him from the log. It was not a gentle pull. The rider was snatched from danger, but with such force that he was thrown clear over the elephant's back.

As the tusker turned toward safer water, he found Boon struggling for the bank. He might have lifted him gently in his trunk, but instead he butted him, slapped him. Sewai felt that Boon deserved the punishment, but he was afraid the man would be drowned. He was powerless to control Poo Rapatanahan, for the elephant had taken matters into his own hands. He pushed the struggling rider under the water, and then jerked him up, only to toss him under again.

It was not until Boon had given up that Poo Rapatanahan lifted him from the water to the shore.

When Nai Kow arrived on the sandbar, Boon was apologizing to Sewai for what he had done. During those awful moments he had realized that he deserved no help from either the boy or Poo Rapatanahan. His apologies were sincere, but Nai Kow interrupted him.

"Sewai," he said, "you are one of the best mahouts in the district. As long as your father is ill, I will expect you to act as Poo Rapatanahan's mahout. And," he added, "I'm indeed proud to have you!"

* * * * *

"The Boy Mahout," by Clark Brockman. Published in St. Nicholas, *September 1930. Original text owned by Joe Wheeler. Clark Brockman wrote for popular magazines during the first half of the twentieth century.*

KINDNESS CONQUERS

Frank Braden

Though the tiger was no longer in the jungle, the jungle was still in the tiger. Attila, a powerful Bengal tiger, was both admired and feared in the circus world. He had killed before—and could again.
But Louis Ross had a plan . . .

* * * * *

Readers will doubtless relate this true story to the worldwide headlines resulting from an ill-fated tiger act known as Siegfried and Roy in Las Vegas.

* * * * *

There is a little town in Michigan—Bad Axe—where they still date the happenings of one season in this fashion: "Yes, that was the year the menagerie tiger got loose."

The coming of the menagerie to Bad Axe was in itself a momentous event, but the escape from its cage of a Royal Bengal tiger—the famous and powerful Attila known throughout the menagerie world as "a killer"—put Bad Axe on the map, so to speak, and gave the village and county residents a red-letter day.

It was high noon. The street parade—two miles of it—had returned to the lot, followed by hundreds of appreciative men, women, boys, and girls. Many of them had driven into town in old-fashioned spring wagons—driven uncertainly, for it had been hard to believe that the big menagerie was really coming to Bad Axe. But the sight of the long strings of cars—stock, elephant, and sleeping cars—on the railway sidings, the sweeping spreads of canvas as the big tent went up, and then the actual passing in review of the impressive street parade reassured them; their holiday was secure.

The last of the six-horse teams had swung under the raised side wall, pulling its cage of wild beasts into place behind the guard ropes. Ladders had been placed against many of the ornate wagons for the descent of the young women who trained and performed with the animals and had ridden through the streets seated on benches atop them. Suddenly someone screamed, "Attila! Attila! He's loose. There, over there—under the lion cage!"

Almost at the same moment menagerie attendants, drivers, horses, and townspeople, peering into the enclosure from beyond the raised side wall, sighted the great, striped beast slinking slowly along.

Pandemonium!

Animal men rushed for steel forks and rolls of side wall. People scattered in terror. Horses reared and snorted, some screeching in their frenzy. Jungle cats, startled, roared. Elephants, straining at newly fastened leg chains, faced toward the escaped killer; their little eyes were glazing red with age-old hate as they trumpeted their readiness for combat.

The little lady who had given the alarm, brave as she usually was, scampered back up the ladder to the top of the hippopotamus den and tried vainly to hurl the ladder aside.

"Here," said a voice, "I'll help you."

She looked down into the blue eyes of a tall, blond youth clad in flannel shirt, corduroy trousers, and laced woodsman's boots. He lifted the ladder away from the den and was turning to lay it against the den wheels when a scream filled the tent. The youth whirled to see the huge tiger, which had leaped twenty feet, bearing to the ground a burro tied in the zebra lines. With its death cry the burro lay still; its back was broken. With the ladder poised over his head, the youth ran toward the tiger as animal men armed with stakes and forks closed warily in. Attila crouched, for the moment nonplused.

"Heads up!" cried the tall youth, and brought the ladder down with a crash on the tiger's head.

The ladder splintered into pieces, but Attila, giant striped killer, relaxed, rolled over on his side, and lay quiet. In an instant the men positioned pieces of side wall around the beast, then heaved him back into his cage, the door of which by some accident had become unlocked.

Chris Zeitz, boss of the menagerie, looked at the strange youth admiringly. "You an animal man?" he asked.

"No, but I've had some experience with bears, moose, deer, and wildcats in the North," answered the boy.

"Want a job?" inquired Chris smilingly.

"Yes—in just a minute," said the boy. He walked over to the polar bear cage, shouldered a ladder, then went over to rescue the girl who was sitting on top of the hippopotamus den watching the dazed eyes of Attila. When she reached the ground, she thanked him, then added, "You're an animal man, aren't you?"

"Yes, miss," he replied and smiled. "I guess I am. Looks like I'm hired. I've always liked animals, the wilder the better, and I'm going to join up with this outfit. Beats the lumber business, I think."

"That's nice," she said and was off to the dressing room and out of this story, which is not a romance, but a narrative of how Louis Ross, a blond woodsman with an understanding of animals, founded a new school of lion, leopard, puma, and jaguar training—a school dedicated to the proposition that all wild animals are "human" under their skins, and, being so, respond willingly to training, submit docilely to man's mastery, once their fears are allayed and their minds grasp what is wanted of them. It is a good school. Its motto is love and kindness, and they have Lou Ross as its dean.

When the new animal man reported for duty the next morning, his first assigned task was cleaning the bear cage. Each time he passed Attila, he winked at him. But the big cat gave no heed. In his greenish-yellow eyes was a faraway look. He had no time for a mere animal, not even if the man *had* broken a ladder over his head the day before. "Never mind, Attila," said Louis to himself. "I talk business to you later."

It was weeks before he had a chance to try his hand at training, but the chance came in public, and therefore was noteworthy. In accepting the offer

to put Prince, a great brown bear, through his paces in the steel arena, Louis underestimated the effect his first public appearance might have on his own nerves. He liked bears, especially Prince, and was confident that he and the friendly old fellow could come through the act with honor. Prince always brought his audience to a fever pitch by standing on the topmost of half a dozen piled-up tables and rocking them slowly back and forth till it seemed to the crowds that every swing must send them all tumbling to the ground, and Prince with them. However, when they did fall, Prince generally reached out and quietly grasped a rope surreptitiously let down by the property owner and descended coolly hand over hand, or rather paw over paw.

Louis had received a new uniform shortly before his appearance. It was a gaudy red-and-gold affair, and he was proud of it. When he stepped smartly to the front of the arena and saluted the audience with a flourish of his cap, he experienced a mighty thrill of pride—and then stage fright seized him. He trembled violently as he began arranging the tables, and Prince, taught to waltz around the cage during that part of the program, hesitated at Louis's uncertain cues. The animal took advantage of Louis's nervousness.

Suddenly Prince reached out and tore at Louis's trousers. Startled, the boy grasped a table and placed it before him. Prince tore it from his grasp, advancing. Louis's voice was gone, and his teeth were chattering. He hastily reached for another table. Prince threw it aside, and the audience was then treated to the spectacle of a frenzied trainer in torn trousers racing here and there for tables while a great bear in sportive mood tore them from his grasp and tried with great glee to rip off his trainer's gay red pantaloons. The crowd roared with laughter. It was the funniest thing that had ever happened at any menagerie!

Then the spirit of Louis Ross revived. He got back his voice. "Prince! Waltz!" he commanded. "Waltz!"

He forced himself to advance, talking himself back into courage. Prince hesitated; then, seeing that the trainer had control of himself, meekly began his dance. The act finished amid cheers.

Louis had learned a great lesson. "Since that day," he says, "I have always had myself in hand when working with animals. A man must be master of himself before trying to master any creature."

Each day Louis held long chats with Attila. The great cat, which had killed one trainer and badly lacerated several, grew to welcome Louis's visits. The tiger would rise and nose along the bars as Louis talked. Chris Zeitz, the manager, often declared that Attila purred when Louis, extremely alert, would venture to stroke his flanks. Finally the boy obtained Chris's permission to enter the cage. It was in Galveston, Texas, where he made the experiment, armed with prod and chair, while Chris himself stood at the end door ready to aid. Animal men and keepers gathered eagerly to watch with anxiety the conquest of Attila, the killer.

The boy talked to the tiger quietly for several minutes and then slipped easily into the cage. For a moment Attila blinked his astonishment at the effrontery; then he set to spring. Talking gently, Louis stood motionless with the chair poised as a shield and the prod ready. The crowd held its breath. Chris had given strict orders against any outcry. With eyes narrowed to yellowish slits, tail swishing ever so slightly, but stiff with the tenseness of gathered muscles, Attila gazed into Louis's eyes. Louis stared unflinchingly into the yellow eyes of the killer, and his talk poured soothingly on. It was a memorable clash of wills. For eight minutes the eyes of man and beast clung, struggling for mastery. Finally Attila's gaze faltered. He relaxed.

Chris outside sighed with relief. "I never saw a cat so near to a spring and give it up," he breathed to an assistant.

Louis called for a stool. It was shoved in to him. He sat down, talking to Attila in the same gentle cadence. Rising, he pushed the chair against the tiger, prodding him until he rose to a sitting posture. Once Attila snarled, lashing at the chair in Louis's hand. The boy laughed. "Good old Attila, my little baby, my pretty little baby," he crooned, and prodded gently. The animal was in the corner, and the prodding could indicate only one thing—the trainer wished him to get up on the stool. Louis saw in the beast's eyes the flash that came with understanding.

An old trainer outside saw it too. "Now's the time to force him!" he exclaimed. "Jab him now. He knows the trick you want. Force him!"

But Louis continued the gentle prodding. Snarling, the tiger began leaping from side to side, madly trying to evade doing what he knew the man wanted him to do. "Here's where I could go the route these other trainers went, Chris," said Louis, "but I'll have him doing this willingly before five minutes, and in public he'll show audiences that he enjoys it—if not beaten into it. Watch!"

Attila ceased leaping. Louis's chair, which had been swinging in arcs before the tiger's nose, became still. Then the trainer closed in slowly with gentle talk; his prod indicated the stool, and then he pushed the beast toward it. For several minutes Attila stood still. Then without warning he clambered onto the stool and sat down.

Louis was exultant. "Good! It's the only way. Look at him! I declare he's grinning! Attila, you old fraud, you're not bad. You're a regular fellow, Attila."

Thus began the famous eighteen-tiger act, as it is known in the menagerie business. Each Royal Bengal actor Louis trained in the same fashion. All of them he taught to ride horses; the instinctive fear that the horses had for the tigers he overcame by keeping them near each other for days, with bars between them, of course. The tigers' instinct to tear the horses to shreds he conquered by watchfulness, by forcing the cats to see that in attacking the horses they attacked him. Many of them leaped on him in the years it took to "break" the act. Once Soudan and Bengal stood with their cheeks pressed against his. It was a trick that Louis did at the opening of his performance to indicate the affection his animals had for him. That night, suddenly, for no cause at all, Soudan turned and sank his fangs through Louis's cheek and jaw. Sick with the pain of it, Louis did not move. Slowly, with all the care of which he was capable, he reached up, gently forced the tiger's jaws apart, and removed from his flesh the cruel fangs. Had he so much as started when Soudan attacked him, Bengal would have torn in. In agony Louis went on with the act. As he stepped from the arena, he fainted. Seven thousand people who had sat in horror through the ordeal rose in their seats and cheered him.

The two tigers have done the trick thousands of times since, and neither has ever made a move to hurt Louis. He did not punish Soudan. "You see, I did not let him know he had hurt me," he explained. "But," he added, laughing, "my face will not be there if he turns again. I keep my hand on the right muscles. I will be the first to move if ever he should try again."

Because Louis Ross has been a pioneer in the kindly school of training wild animals, he has sometimes suffered for his forbearance; in fact, he bears forty-two jagged scars on his body, including the disfiguring ridge that Soudan's attack left in his cheek.

For years the blond young ex-woodsman presented twenty-seven full-grown African lions in a spectacular act, easily the largest group that has been presented in America within two decades. During the performance one night, the two largest lions, Samson and Kaiser, sprang at each other without preliminary ado. Kaiser bowled the trainer over as he leaped at Samson. In an instant all the twenty-seven lions were fighting fiercely in the arena—a writhing, biting, slashing mass of jungle kings, with Louis completely out of sight beneath. It took the entire force of animal men ten minutes to stop the combat, for no man dared enter the arena. With long steel bars and firebrands, they worked feverishly from outside the big cage.

Meanwhile they were sure that Louis was being torn to ribbons. But the young man had remained cool. As he fell beneath the tidal wave of battling beasts, he turned face downward and lay motionless. The action saved his life, for when the lions were at last driven into the runway leading from the arena, the rescuers picked the trainer up unconscious, badly cut in twenty places, but very much alive.

When he revived, he laughed. "You see, it was a gentlemen's quarrel," he said whimsically, "and it was up to me to see fair play and not to interfere. I was the referee, and I was keeping score." He looked at his cruelly lacerated arms and body a bit ruefully. "Queer scoreboard!" he concluded.

Louis did not punish Samson and Kaiser, but for days he gave them extra rehearsals together, and instantly quelled the slightest exhibition of resentment either might make toward the other, until he was assured that they understood what the extra work was for. "See how simple it is!" he exclaimed. "Samson understands, Kaiser understands, and they both know I understand. We are working and progressing in unison. It's solid ground we're covering. It's more than animal training—it's animal education!"

One day Attila, leaping savagely for his dinner as the menagerie attendants pushed a meaty bone under the bars, broke a big molar off at the gum. Louis saw that a dental operation was immediately necessary, for the great tiger bit fiercely on the snagged tooth to combat the pain. Louis had the cage pulled into the open, where the light was good. Over and over he told Attila that he would not hurt him. Soothingly he talked as he made ready lassos to lift over the tiger's paws in order to draw his legs under him and pull him to the bars, where the dental work could be done. Attila understood that his master meant no harm, but he was no more in favor of a session in a dentist's chair than is a small boy. In spite of Louis's reassuring flow of words, it was a tedious, though exciting task to throw the loops over the tiger's paws. Time and again Ross succeeded, only to have the panic-stricken beast rear and elude the tightening lariat. Spectators stood and admired the supreme patience of the trainer. Not once did Louis's voice betray the exasperation he must have felt.

After thirty minutes, when even the spectators were exhausted with the strain, the trainer managed to loop the fore feet and draw them together. The hind feet were then fastened, and the animal thrown. After that Attila seemed to take it for granted that Louis knew best. He made no outcry, no move, as Louis, after passing loops about the lower and upper jaws to force the mouth open, went swiftly and expertly to work with forceps and knife and cotton. What had a few minutes before seemed impossible became absurdly simple. The sight of the great, striped creature lying there so quietly could not but impress the most thoughtless. Here was a giant Royal Bengal tiger, a notorious killer before he became a pupil of Louis Ross, submitting to a painful operation without the slightest remonstrance; he understood that his master was taking the only means of helping him.

Quickly the trainer finished the job, and quickly Attila was on his feet, licking his maw placidly, seemingly with relief. "Come here, Attila! Come to me, my baby!" called Louis. And the tiger came. "My nice big boy, my pet. It's all right now, isn't it, Attila?" whispered the trainer, stroking the flanks of the beautiful creature.

There was no doubt about it. Chris Zeitz was right. Attila, one-time killer, but now a thoroughly educated and dignified performer, purred—purred like a house cat!

* * * * *

"Kindness Conquers," by Frank Braden. Published in The Youth's Instructor, *January 20, 1925. Printed by permission of Joe Wheeler (P.O. Box 1246, Conifer, CO 80433) and Review and Herald® Publishing Association. Frank Braden wrote for popular magazines during the first half of the twentieth century.*

THE SMALLEST BIRD IN THE WORLD

Alice May

It was in the intolerable midday heat of Jamaica, one never-to-be-forgotten day in the pre-air-conditioning 1870s, that a visitor to the island heard a voice she'd never heard before.

Just what was it that was too important to wait until her siesta was over?

* * * * *

In a favorite niche in my room, adorned with my choicest specimens of ferns and plumy grasses, hangs, suspended from two slight twigs of bamboo, a tiny, daintily fashioned bird's nest.

Around this small nest cluster many and grateful memories of the fairy-like owner, a vervain hummingbird, smallest of all known birds, and the most charming and best loved pet I ever possessed. Many a weary hour, during the almost intolerable heat of midday in Jamaica, has been charmed away by the joyous, exuberant life and wild, merry ways of my little feathered pet.

The day I obtained possession of this bit of bird-kind, I remember as being warmer and more unbearable than usual. I had been all the morning lying in my hammock, with jalousies tightly drawn to exclude the blinding rays of the sun outside, vainly trying to find relief in a vigorous fanning by my maid, Justina, and in cooling drinks of iced lime juice, when my attention was drawn to the sound of a dispute on the piazza outside, and some languid curiosity was excited by the oft-repeated words, "I've got a tiny bird for the missy."

Although, during the midday in Jamaica, neither business nor pleasure was often allowed to interfere with the important task of keeping cool, I had enough energy left to demand that the owner of the voice be admitted.

In shuffled a boy, ducking his head at every step, showing the whitest of teeth, and carrying something carefully covered in a tattered rag that I supposed was intended for a hat.

"Tiny bird, fly very fast; will the missy peek at him?"

Now, that hat was certainly an objectionable article to peek into, but peek I did, and was rewarded by seeing what seemed to be the remains of a dirty gauze net.

I drew back and eyed the boy with stern indignation, but the confident, upraised face, with its grin of expectancy, induced me to venture one more peek. And this time I was more successful, for, wrapped in the folds of gauze, I espied so tiny a ball of ruffled feathers that I could not believe it was an entire bird. But upon carefully extricating this small mass of green and black plumage, I discovered it to be the tiniest bird I ever saw in my life, but now limp and lifeless.

"Why, my boy," exclaimed I, "this poor bird is dead. What can I do with it?"

The boy's face fell, and the grin faded.

"That tiny bird was alive when I put him in the hat."

During this conversation, I had been holding the small bird in my warm palm, and now, much to my surprise, I felt a slight quiver in the little frame.

I held the tiny creature to my lips and gently breathed upon it, and soon a feeble fluttering of the wings, and a faint *cree, cree* assured me that the wee thing still had a little life in it.

"Warra," cried the boy, "him alive now, for sure. Missy put the breath in him."

I hurriedly dispatched Justina for sweetened water, for my birdie was rapidly regaining strength, and I was anxious to reassure the timid, fluttering heart.

The sweetened water forthcoming, I put a few drops between my lips and

carefully pressed the little beak against them, and after a slight struggle I felt it sip, feebly at first, then eagerly, at the sweet drops. Soon after, my prisoner was struggling to escape.

From that moment my heart was won, and it was with real joy that I saw my bird dart suddenly from my hand and, alighting on the edge of a picture frame, commence a vigorous preening of his disordered plumage.

"Will missy want the other little birdie on the nest?" inquired the boy.

I then learned that this bird was the male, which the boy had succeeded in catching by means of an old ring net, left by some naturalist in this land teeming with insect life, and the female was still in the nest, on an old plantation bearing the queer name of Bozzetty Hall, situated near the remarkable river of "One-stick-over-the-one-eye." The boy's own settlement of shanties was called Harmony Pens, while he himself rejoiced in the unlikely name of Snowball.

I gladly consented to take the other bird and nest, if he could obtain them, and handing him the desired money, I sent him on his way rejoicing.

My whole mind was now given to the taming of my pet, which I knew was a vervain hummingbird, a native of Jamaica, and the smallest of even his tiny race. The name *vervain* probably originated from these birds being so often found hovering over the blue blossoms of the West Indian vervain, a plant common in all the fields and pastures of Jamaica.

The rather commonplace English name of hummingbird is quite misapplied in the case of the vervain, as the name comes from the humming sound made by the wings in the rapid flight. But with the vervain, this sound, from its diminutive size and wonderful velocity, is more like the sharp *whir-r-r* of insect wings. Indeed, from a distance, darting from flower to flower, the tiny creature looks very like a bumblebee. Some of the natives of Jamaica apply extremely fanciful names to these aerial gems, our hummingbirds, such as "tresses of the daystar," "rays of the sun," and "murmuring birds." The French name, *Oiseau-mouche* (bird-fly), is quite applicable to my fairy bird, as he was literally fly sized, hardly larger than a locust, being only an inch and a quarter from his quarter-inch, needlelike beak to his small ten-feathered tail, which, like the beak, was held high in the air in the most aggressive way you can imagine.

His head was the size of a pea, and the bright, beadlike eyes were capable of seeing objects almost invisible to us, for I could see him snap his little bill and swallow as with real zest some flying insect not visible to my unaided eyes.

His legs, hardly longer than a good-sized mosquito's, were wonderfully strong, the funny little claws clinging so closely to a string or twig that one feared to use the force necessary to disengage them. This hummingbird is not as brilliantly colored as some others, but his plumage shines with a metallic luster that, in the sunlight, is dazzling, particularly after preening every feather, as he is very fond of doing, being an extremely vain little fellow.

But I must tell you how I succeeded in making this strange wild creature contented and happy with his new mistress and prison house.

My first thought was of a cage, for soon the jalousies must be raised to admit the cool evening breeze, and my windows, with most others in this tropical climate, were without glass, depending upon drawn jalousies, a kind of lattice blind, with the piazza extending entirely around the house, and also protected by jalousies, for keeping out the wind and rain when these were too boisterous.

I well knew that, at the first opportunity, those rapidly moving wings would bear their little owner out into the free air he loved so well. A cage must be made at once, and my ingenuity was taxed to provide one dainty enough for so exquisite an occupant.

One of the boys about the place, an ingenious fellow, succeeded in wiring together a small frame of bamboo twigs. Bureau drawers were ransacked for a covering, and finally a strong but transparent piece of white gauze was discovered; this was stretched tightly across the frame, leaving one side to be raised or lowered at pleasure. Furniture was then supplied, in the shape of a silver wire and twig of lantana, for sleeping and perching purposes. I then begged a toy cup from my hostess's little daughter, which I filled with the juice of the sugarcane, setting a small quill in it, for the convenience of my guest's tapered beak. I was gazing with extreme complacency upon this contrivance, when Justina innocently remarked that "the little bird thinks that's a flower." I looked at Justina with consternation. Certainly that china cup with the quill inserted did not look like any flower I had ever seen.

However, I placed it in the cage upon my table, in hopes that the cute little fellow would in some way get an inkling of its intended use.

All this time, during the confusion attending the erection of his dwelling, Minim, as I had decided to call this smallest of small birds, was darting about, making himself quite at home, and often visiting a bouquet on my table, composed of sprays of lovely orange blossoms and fragrant bunches of the moringa. As he became bolder, he flashed hither and thither with such startling rapidity that I fairly held my breath. Flying directly from one object to another was quite too tame for this small sprite. Various maneuvers were necessary to enable him to reach the honey cups of moringa. After rapidly circling for some minutes around the table, he would suddenly become stationary over the flowers, suspended on wings vibrating with such extraordinary rapidity that he seemed to be enveloped in mist; then, perhaps, he would make another swift journey about the room before sipping the nectar contained in the fragrant blossoms.

But I began to hear gay voices outside; it was time for the usual afternoon drive, and oh dear! my linen dress hung in limp folds, and the room was so unbearably close that I could hardly breathe, but I dared not raise the jalousies, for by this time my heart was fixed upon keeping my bird. In vain I used every means to entice the cunning little fellow into the birdhouse, sent all the flowers from the room, but a few blossoms which I scattered in the cage. I even cut off the base of one of the flowers and fitted the remainder over the cup of sweets, which it entirely concealed. Minim refused to be enticed by that fraud, and I resigned myself with a sigh to a slate of *déshabillé* for the rest of the evening, for, with neither air nor light, I had not the requisite energy for making a toilet. Minim soon decided to retire for the night and perched upon his favorite picture frame. Through the gathering darkness, I could just see the queer little mite, his beadlike eyes closed, and his head not under his wing, but held a little toward one side, over his shoulder.

I sent Justina to request that my evening meal be served in my room, and also ventured to ask for a dim light, by which I might safely convey my food to my mouth. As the light entered the room, Minim started in terror, fluttered blindly from his perch, and in his endeavors to escape, beat his little body so violently against the wall that he fell to the floor. I ran and picked him up, fearing he was dead, but found that he clung tightly to my hand. I quickly put out the unfortunate light, groped my way to the cage, and succeeded in getting the little claws on to the silver wire, where they clung in desperation. I carefully drew my hand from the cage, lowered the gauze curtain, and listened intently, but there was no sound. So I resigned myself to darkness, and quietly retired to my couch, hoping for better luck on the morrow.

With the first break of dawn I was aroused from my slumber by a sound near me, and, listening, I distinguished a faint song, a plaintive bird-song, feeble but wonderfully sweet. I held my breath with astonishment and delight.

The singer could not be my new pet. Whoever heard a hummingbird make more than a sharp chirp!

The song continuing, I crept softly to the cage, and saw Minim perched upon the twig of lantana, his head raised in bird ecstasy, while pouring forth from the small throat came a continuous sound of faint but exquisite melody.

I had never before obtained so good a view of this wonderful little creature, and I now gazed long with admiration. The swelling breast was covered with fine white feathers, each feather tipped with bright green; the quivering wings were a deep, velvety black, and as a ray of the rising sun struck across the lustrous metallic green of his back and sides, I thought him the loveliest thing I had ever beheld.

The elfin sound continued for ten minutes or more, then ceased, and the bird resumed his brisk, alert air and incessant watch for small stray flies. I began to think the song had been all a dream, but every morning after that, Minim woke me with the sweet song that, of all hummingbirds, is only allowed to the vervain.

Minim soon began to hover about the faded flowers in his cage, evidently with dissatisfaction. I eagerly watched the drooping blossom covering my cup of sweets. Minim, after trying one and another of the flowers, thrust his sharp beak into the flowery cheat, and there the little fellow remained, and I saw with gladness the tiny pumping apparatus within the beak moving at a great rate. What a greedy elf he was! Even after I removed the flower from the cup, he hovered over it every moment, drinking deeply of the sweet juice. I think he considered the whole affair a good invention.

I could fill a volume with the pranks with which this charming little bird amused me during my stay in Jamaica. He grew more joyous and full of life every day, showing no signs of fear, and when allowed his freedom in the room, in search of the necessary insect food, voluntarily returned to his cage and much loved syrup cup.

I easily taught him to sip from my lips, and often have I been roused from my midday siesta by sharp, angry cries, and an eager little beak pecking at my lips, in search of the sweet drops often found there.

His curiosity was funny to see. All my garments had to undergo a thorough investigation, and my hair was made to stand on end, with his frantic endeavors to obtain my hair ribbons. The many-colored bows adorning Justina's head seemed to excite his indignation, and I have laughed till the tears came, to see the poor girl trying in vain to escape the attacks of her little persecutor; and when the sharp claws became entangled in her mass of hair, her indignation would vent itself in a shower of abuse possible only to a genuine Jamaican.

Not only did my wee birdie possess an amusing amount of vanity and birdlike self-conceit, but within the diminutive frame was a spirit capable of the most valorous deeds. Indeed, the little fellow was really pugnacious and often reminded me of a small bantam cock.

Ancient Mexicans believed that the souls of departed warriors inhabited the bodies of hummingbirds. Surely, if this myth were true, the spirit of some great chieftain lived again in the frail body of my pet.

One morning a mango hummingbird came flashing through the open window. I quickly lowered the jalousies and opened Minim's cage, hoping to obtain possession of my lovely guest.

Minim, of course, darted from the cage; he eyed the magnificent stranger for some time with apparent serenity, but suddenly, without warning, darted toward him with a perfect shriek of rage, and for a moment all I could see was a confused, rapidly revolving mass of feathers. First the mango, then Minim, would be uppermost in this terrific combat. I was bitterly repenting my rash act, for the mango was much the larger bird and I feared would kill my pet, when I saw the stranger bird fall to the ground. I hurried to him and found that he was nearly dead, while Minim began quietly pluming himself with an air of calm superiority. I never tried that experiment again, although I am sure my little pugilist was capable of whipping a fellow twice his size.

Little Snowball one day brought me the female bird and nest. Minim made charming husbandly advances to his little wife, but madame, refusing to be comforted, drooped her small head and died. Her volatile husband refused to perform a parent's duties, and to this day I have two pearly white eggs, lying in a nest no larger than an English walnut divided transversely. It is a wonderful, compact little cup, made of the white soft down in the ripened pods of the cotton tree, the silky fibers tightly held together with some sticky substance, probably the saliva of the bird. Minute spiderwebs are closely interwoven around the outside of the nest, and here and there are stuck bright bits of green and gray lichens, making altogether a wonderfully pretty little birdhouse.

As the time drew near when I must leave the island, I was troubled about the fate of my pet. I feared for the frail life during the long, rough voyage, and I had no friend in Jamaica with whom I could trust the little creature; so I finally decided that the greatest kindness I could render my tiny friend would be to give him his liberty.

The last morning dawned. Minim, as usual, gave me vigorous help in arranging my hair, became entangled in my hat ribbons, and pecked at my crimps. For the last time I held the dear fellow to my face and felt the eager bill searching for sweet syrup between my lips. Then, with a heavy heart, I went to the window, raised the jalousies, gave my pet one little farewell squeeze, and opened wide my hands.

With one wild, joyous dash of fluttering wings and a sharp *screep* of delight, my ungrateful little hummingbird sprang forth to meet the fresh morning air, and the last I saw of Minim was a small flashing bit of green and black feathers rapidly dashing a way from my sorrowful gaze, growing smaller and smaller in the distance, until it was lost in a wilderness of waving palms and brilliant, luxuriant tropical foliage.

My beautiful Minim had returned to the wild, sunny freedom from which he had been taken.

* * * * *

"The Smallest Bird in the World," by Alice May. Published in St. Nicholas, *April 1881. Original text owned by Joe Wheeler. Alice May wrote for turn-of-the-twentieth-century magazines.*

ANDROCLES AND THE LION

Author Unknown

Perhaps the most famous true story having to do with lions (outside of Holy Writ) is this one, as chronicled by an editor of Chatterbox *magazine.*

* * * * *

The story of Androcles and the lion is told by Dion Cassius, a Roman historian of undoubted veracity. Androcles was the slave of a noble Roman who was proconsul of Afric, or Africa. He had been found guilty of a fault for which his master was going to put him to death, but he found an opportunity to escape and fled into the deserts of Numidia. As he was wandering among the barren sands, and almost dead with heat and thirst, he saw a cave in a rock. Finding just at the entrance a stone to sit upon, which was shaded from the fierce heat of the sun, he rested for some time.

At length, to his great surprise, a huge overgrown lion stood before him, and seeing him, immediately walked toward him. Androcles gave himself up for lost; but the lion, instead of treating him as he expected, laid his right paw on his lap, and with a low moan of pain licked his hand. Androcles, after having recovered himself a little from his fright, plucked up courage enough to look at the paw which was laid on his lap and observed a large thorn in it. He

immediately pulled it out, and by squeezing it very gently made a great deal of poisonous blood and matter run out, which probably freed the lion from the great pain he was in. The lion again licked his hand, and with a brighter look in his eyes left him, soon returning, however, with a fawn he had just killed. This he laid down at the feet of his benefactor and went off again in pursuit of more prey, not limping now as he did when Androcles first saw him, but bounding along as if his paw had never had anything the matter with it.

Androcles, after having subsisted upon the fawn and other food which the lion brought him for several days, at length got tired of this frightful solitude and savage companionship, expecting that at any moment the lion might forget his act of kindness and devour him. So he resolved to deliver himself into his master's hands and suffer the worst effects of his displeasure.

Now his master, as was customary for the proconsul of Africa, was at that time collecting together a present of all the largest lions that could be found in the country in order to send them to Rome, that they might furnish a show for the Roman people, and upon Androcles his slave surrendering himself, he ordered him to be carried to Rome as soon as the lions were sent there, and that for his crime he should be exposed to fight one of the lions in the amphitheater for the pleasure of the people.

This was all carried into effect. Androcles, after having been alone in the wilderness, with the probability of being torn to pieces by lions, was now before a multitude of people, in the arena, looking forward to the same dreadful death.

At length a huge lion bounded out from the place where it had been kept hungry for the show. He was in great rage, and in one or two great leaps he advanced toward Androcles, who was in the center of the arena, with a short sword in his hand. But suddenly the lion stopped, regarded him with a wistful look, and letting his tail droop, crept quietly toward him and licked and caressed his feet. Androcles, after a short pause of great surprise, discovered that it was his old Numidian friend, and immediately renewed his acquaintance with him.

Their obvious friendship made little sense to the excited beholders, but after hearing an account of the whole affair from Androcles, they urged the emperor to pardon him. The emperor did so and gave into his possession the lion, who, because he'd once been kindly treated, had saved his benefactor's life.

Androcles kept the lion and treated him well in return for the food the faithful animal had obtained for him in the desert and for having saved his life.

Dion Cassius, the great historian, says that he himself saw Androcles leading the lion through the streets of Rome (and his word is not to be doubted), the people gathering about them and saying to one another, "This is the lion who was the man's host; this is the man who was the lion's physician."

* * * * *

"Androcles and the Lion," author unknown. Published in 1890 Chatterbox. *Original text owned by Joe Wheeler.*

LODI OF THE VELDT

Samuel Scoville, Jr.

Only a mother's desperate love for her kits would have caused the bush cat (known to biologists as a tiger cat or serval) to risk a lion's wrath. The price paid was swift—and final.

Only one of her cubs was saved by the Afrikaner Baas Vogel. Little did he then realize that luck was fickle: one day he'd have it, another and it would be gone—and that the bush cat he'd named Lodi would represent the difference.

* * * * *

Slowly, gray-black thorn trees deepened to ashy silver, the flaming African stars paled, and the lilac of the sky changed to violet. Then the full moon wheeled above the baobab trees, which stood here and there upon the plain like lurking monsters. At first it was a pale, pale bubble of light, then a shield of burnished gold, to hang at last in mid sky an incandescent mass of white fire, which made lanes of light through deep *dongas* and *kloof* alike. Deceived by the false dawn, hornbills began to mourn from the thickets, and the hollow, liquid crooning of little wood doves sounded from the mango trees.

Suddenly, in that strange, still moonlight that had the trick of transmuting all colors into charcoal and old silver, there sounded a wailing cry, *M-wa,*

m-wa, m-wa. The next moment a long-legged cat with glaring eyes and an orange-tawny coat blotched with black stood in the veldt and sniffed the air hungrily.

Rarely enough does that bush cat, the serval, appear in the open. That one, however, had special reasons for being bold—four, round, chubby ones denned in a hollow limb of a yellow-wood tree. Wherefore, when her unerring nostrils brought the news that a lion had killed a sassaby, that swiftest of all antelopes, and cached its carcass back of a big mimosa bush, she came out to investigate.

Ordinarily, that tiger cat would no more have ventured to interfere with a lion's kill than she would have crossed the ten-foot deadline that surrounds a rock python in coil or entered the haunted waters of one of those rivers in which crocodiles lurk. Hunting, however, had been bad with the spotted cat the night before, and the double task of nursing and guarding her cubs made it necessary for her to secure food at once. So with every muscle tense, ready to vanish like the shadow of a flickering leaf at the first sign of danger, she crept foot by foot toward the spot where the half-eaten body of the buck was hidden.

As she came nearer to the bush, her nose caught a hot, raw reek, and that little alarm bell that beats for all of the wild folk clanged, "Lion! Lion! Lion!" against her brain. Perhaps it was the fierce hunger which gnawed at her like a rat that made her disregard that warning for the first and last time in her life. With staring eyes she searched every shadow before she crept in toward the torn carcass, but even her flaming gaze could not see the tawny death that lay hidden in the yellow grass. With the terrible craft of his clan, the lion crouched beside his kill to make an example of any of the lesser breeds who dared to molest it.

The strained, lithe figure of the cat crept forward until, with a little growl of satisfaction, the serval sank her teeth deep into a haunch of the dead buck. As if her touch had released some fatal spring, there was the flash of a great paw, and a second later the spotted body of the bush cat lay stiffening beside the plum-colored one of the sassaby—a warning to all jungle thieves to beware the kill of their king.

Yet death still lurked in that thicket, unsated with his double toll. As the lion lay down again in the hollow that his body had made in the long grass, the little figure of a man, scarce four feet high, showed for a moment in the moonlight. The pale yellow skin, gaunt frame, and scanty hair growing in peppercorn tufts, marked him as a Bushman, one of that race of tiny warriors who drove out the men of the Stone Age who first peopled South Africa. In spite of their size, the Bushmen are among the best and bravest hunters in the world, for they alone dare to ambush the lion in his lair or beside his kill and slay him for the sake of his skin and the glory of the deed.

That particular pygmy, washed in a decoction of wild cassia so that the lion might not scent him, had lain since sunset hidden near the dead antelope, waiting with the inexhaustible patience of his kind for the great cat to show some sign of his presence. Armed only with a small, weak bow and unfeathered reed arrows with bone heads, it seemed impossible that he would dare to attack the king of beasts—yet the Bushman never hesitated. There was a twang from the bushes where he stood and an arrow buzzed through the air like a bee and pierced the lion's tawny shoulder. With a growl the great cat snapped at the arrow, breaking it off short, but leaving the bone head imbedded in his flesh. The little hunter did not shoot again, but crouched down in the thicket to wait, knowing that nothing living could long survive the stab of an arrow point that had been thrust into the body of a devil-caterpillar and then smeared with the gum of the poison tree.

For long minutes the lion gave no sign. Then he suddenly stood up and, towering to his full height, gave that dreadful, full-throated roar that shatters the air like a clap of thunder. The great body swayed slightly where it stood, the fierce eyes blazed with a yellow flame, and with another tremendous roar, the king of all the killers of the veldt pitched over—dead.

All that night, four soft, woolly little serval cubs waited in vain for their mother to come back. The next day three of them cried loudly from hunger. The fourth cub did not cry at all. By midafternoon when his mother had not appeared, he thrust his round head out of the hollow limb and tried to climb down the tree, whereupon he promptly lost his balance and pitched to the ground below. There Baas Vogel found him while on his way across the veldt to his plantation, the largest in that part of South Africa. Though faint and frightened and shaken by his fall, the serval kitten faced the old Boer bravely, hunching up his back and giving tiny growls as a warning of the terrible things he would do if molested.

Baas Vogel was much amused.

"Come you home with me, little rascal," he said, in the peculiar brand of

English which he always insisted upon using. "It may be that thou shalt help kill some of those greedy cane rats that eat up my crops so fast as I sow them."

By the time the Boer reached the plantation, the little tiger cat was too weak to stand, for he had been a night and a day without food. It was evident that unless he was fed at once the last fierce spark of life which he had left would flicker out. There was no milk in the house, nor any other food suitable for an unweaned kitten, and no one seemed to know what to do. At that critical moment, Spot, the house cat, happened to be crossing the veranda on her way to where a litter of kittens was waiting for her. Purring loudly, with her tail arched high above her back, she pushed her way contemptuously through the group of helpless humans, stood over the starving cub, and in another moment was nursing that orphan of the veldt as if he were one of her own kittens.

From that day the serval cat became an important member of the plantation household. Tali, the native overseer, christened him "Lodi," which in his Bechuana tongue meant "Luck."

Under Spot's nursing the stranger grew apace and was weaned long before her own kittens. The first that the plantation knew of Lodi's change of diet was one morning when he followed Baas Vogel into the poultry yard. As a flock of pigeons settled on the ground to pick up the strewn grain, Lodi, who had hidden behind the Boer's great bulk, sprang at one bound clear across his master's head and landed like the little tiger he was among the feeding birds. Before the flock could take to flight, he had struck down no less than four with swift, dabbing strokes of his armed paws. That was the end of Lodi's liberty for many a long day, for thereafter he was kept on a chain.

A few months later and he had grown into a magnificent cat, two feet high at the shoulder, while his lithe, orange-colored body, inked with round black spots, was a good three feet long, and his ringed tail accounted for another foot. He had eyes like flaming topazes, and his feet and pads were shrimp-pink.

Sometimes, as a special treat, the Baas would take him out on the veldt unchained to hunt for himself. Long-legged, lithe, and lean, it was a pleasure to the old Boer to watch the incredible speed and certainty with which his pet would catch field mice and cane rats. Before long he was stalking nobler quarry. Once the two walked into a covey of partridges, and as they whirred up from the grass, Lodi sprang six feet into the air and caught one in midflight, although an African partridge, like his American relative, buzzes through the air like a bullet. Another day, Lodi saw a bush pigeon preening itself on a nearby tree. Crouching low, the serval slipped along the ground like a snake, taking advantage of every bit of cover, his tawny body blending perfectly with the yellow grass and dry fern about him. Crouching until almost flat on the ground, the great cat suddenly shot up fully ten feet straight into the air, snatched the bird off the limb, and brought it back to the Boer to be broiled for luncheon.

Then came the unlucky day when in his master's absence, old Tali took Lodi hunting. In the late afternoon, when the trees that fringed the horizon were etched in inky purple against a blazing orange sky, the two plodded homeward empty-handed through the cool green light.

Suddenly, out of a great reed-bed full of golden finches and malachite sunbirds burst a blue duiker, smallest of all South African antelope and only about the size of a hare. So fast did he move that he showed only as a blue-brown blur against the yellow grass. Instantly, a tawny streak shot toward him, and before the startled Tali could stop him, the serval cat was gone. In vain Tali gave the long wailing cry of the bush cat with which he was accustomed to call Lodi back. There was a crackling of the reeds, a waving of distant ferns, and the little duiker racing for his life and the tiger cat hard at his heels had both disappeared. Tali hunted and called until dark before he returned home and reported the loss of the old Boer's pet.

Baas Vogel was greatly incensed at the news.

"Big dunce," he thundered, "be off early tomorrow and come not back without my Lodi, or I break every bone in thy worthless body!"

As always, the old Boer's bark was worse than his bite, but the Bechuana took the threat seriously. Early the next day, with his tin billy and a sack of mealie-meal, he disappeared into the veldt.

For the whole of a long day he quartered back and forth, mile after mile over the plain, hunting and calling for the lost Lodi. There was no sight of the serval until late in the afternoon, when there was a sudden rustle in the reeds near the old man, and out into the open sprang Lodi with the dead duiker flung across his shoulder. Bechuana and the bush cat returned to the plantation in triumph, and the Boer was so pleased over his pet's exploit in running down a blue duiker that he not only forgave the old native, but presented him with an extra ration of snuff to make up for his hard words of the day before.

Baas Vogel's joy over the return of the prodigal was somewhat tempered by an incident which happened a few days after Lodi came back. He had been placed on a chain outside of an enclosure screened by wide-meshed wire intended to protect the poultry from any more of his sudden attacks. One old rooster, an imported white Wyandotte, used to exasperate Lodi by thrusting his head through the screen and stealing scraps.

One morning Lodi's food dish happened to be placed less than a foot from the netting. Watching his chance, the white cock would thrust his head through the screen and snatch up bits from the plate. Hissing with rage, the serval each time sprang at the Wyandotte, but the old rooster had calculated the length of the chain to an inch, and at every spring the tiger cat was jerked painfully back, while the thief went on calmly gobbling up his dinner.

After a third unsuccessful attempt, Lodi ostentatiously gave up all hopes of catching his unwelcome visitor. Crouching down as close to the dish as the chain would permit, he closed his eyes and, doubling up his paws beneath him, apparently went to sleep under the shade of a pyramid cypress tree that towered above him, black-green against the summer sky.

The old rooster eyed him suspiciously for some time. At last he pretended to thrust his head in and pick at the plate. The tiger cat did not move or even open his eyes. Half a dozen times the crafty cock repeated this feint with no sign of life from Lodi. At last, evidently convinced that the big serval was really asleep, the rooster poked his head clear through the mesh, snatched a morsel from the plate and gulped it down, chuckling deep in his throat as he did so. Again he repeated the theft. When for the third time his red comb and wattles dipped into the dish, a long spotted paw shot out like a flash, and the next instant the cock's headless body was trembling about, decapitated instantly by the cat's keen, retractile claws.

The Baas exploded with a loud report when the news came to him of the passing of his prize Wyandotte.

"Wicked little spotted imp!" he thundered. "First it is that you run away and my best man loses for me a day's work. Then you pull from his body off, the head of my fine big white rooster who is worth a thousand bush cats. Now I fix you!"

Lodi only blinked his gooseberry-green eyes and rubbed his head disarmingly against the Baas's leg. His caresses availed him nothing, for the next day he was shut up in a cage made of close-meshed wire and no longer allowed to run about the enclosure even on a chain. Those cramped quarters soon had a bad effect upon his temper, and before long he would snarl whenever anyone approached. One morning, Kosi, the boy whose duty it was to clean out Lodi's cage, teased the fretting animal with his broom. The serval hissed murderously, but the boy kept on until, with a growl that sounded like the rasping of rough iron, the tiger cat sprang through the half-open door, dodged the broom that the boy flourished in front of him, and, like the flash of a brandished blade, sprang for Kosi's throat. If Baas Vogel had not happened to be passing just at that moment, the furious animal would have killed his tormentor. It was old Tali who secured the acquittal of his pet.

"With my own eyes," he testified, "I saw that worthless lump of a boy poke the spotted one with his broom. The evil son of an aardvark deserved far worse than he got."

It had been Spot who had first saved Lodi's life, and it was the last and least of her kittens who secured his liberty for her foster child.

That kitten was a tiny mite of a thing, black as a blot of ink, except for a snubby white nose. The first time that she chanced to wander near Lodi's cage, it was a case of love at first sight with her. Running up to the netting, with tail arched high, she mewed and tried in vain to rub her snowy nose against the tiger cat's black one. Lodi growled furiously and would have killed her instantly if he had been able to reach her. Undiscouraged by this reception, Blackie kept on making friendly advances, until at last Lodi responded to her untiring efforts and the great cat and the tiny kitten would lie for hours at a time as close to each other as the wire netting would allow, crooning and purring as if carrying on long conversations in cat fashion.

At other times they would play games together, leaping around on different sides of the netting and occasionally pretending to dart at each other through the wire meshes.

At last, one day, old Tali opened the door carefully and set the kitten inside. Lodi advanced with arched back, purring loudly, and leaped delightedly up and down and over and around his visitor in a great demonstration of delight. Then he lay down and gently licked Blackie all over with his long, rough tongue, burrowing his nose into her soft fur caressingly.

When at last Tali tried to take the kitten out, the tiger cat instantly gripped Blackie by the loose skin at the back of her neck as a mother cat might, and, throwing a protecting paw around her, gave such a murderous growl that Tali instantly decided to leave the kitten where she was.

From that moment Lodi became a changed character. He growled no more at visitors nor yowled through the night, and the hens and ducks fed about his cage unaffrighted. Before long his conduct became so irreproachable that the Baas decided to give him once more the freedom of the plantation. Accordingly one morning, accompanied by the kitten, Lodi left the cage free and unchained.

Blackie, in spite of her youth, had been properly brought up by Spot in all the traditions of a well-trained house cat, and, in some way known only to herself, soon convinced her companion that pigeons and poultry were to be regarded as allies and not enemies.

Lodi made up for his enforced virtue during the day by his activities at night in the Dene, that wooded strip of jungle surrounding the plantation. There and on the adjacent veldt he would hunt night after night, always bringing his kill through an open window into his master's bedroom for the latter's inspection and approval. Sometimes it was a cane rat big as a rabbit or a rock dassie or a six-pound spring hare, which jumps like a kangaroo and bites like a demon. Whatever his catch, Lodi would crouch with it beside the Baas's bed and purr like a coffee mill until the latter woke up and patted and praised him, whereupon he would depart through the open window, taking his catch with him.

Then there came the fatal night when he caught a striped muishond. The muishond is Africa's reply to the challenge of the American skunk, and though dead, a muishond speaketh—loudly. When Lodi brought that one into the bedroom, the Baas left it at one jump, burying his face in his pillow as he went, not to return until the room had been scrubbed and fumigated over and over again. That unfortunate occurrence was the last straw that broke the back of his patience.

"That bush cat, he leaves now!" he spluttered as soon as he could get his breath.

"Send him not away," pleaded Tali. "The spotted one is a luck cat."

"Yes—a *bad*-luck cat," returned the Baas, grimly. "First it is my pigeons and then my big rooster and now me myself. Luck cat or no, he goes!"

Wherefore the next day Lodi left by train in a covered basket, from which came indignant yowls, on his way to another plantation two hundred miles down the coast.

The Baas missed the great cat more than he had supposed possible. Night after night he would wake with a start, thinking that he heard Lodi's resonant purr beside his bed, or would find himself expecting to feel his lithe body rub against him as he walked across the plantation. Always, however, there was neither sight nor sound of his lost pet.

At last, muishonds or no muishonds, the Baas could stand Lodi's absence no longer and traveled clear down to the other plantation to bring him back, only to find that he had disappeared from his new home the day after his arrival there. He went back without his cat, feeling remorsefully that perhaps he had driven away forever the luck of the plantation, as Tali had said.

The night after his return was a peculiarly stifling one even for South Africa, and it was only after long tossings on his hot pillow that he at length fell into a troubled sleep, to be suddenly awakened by a curious, rubbery thud on the matting by the open window, as if someone had dropped there a piece of heavy garden hose. For a moment the Baas thought that Lodi had come back, but the sound was entirely different from the light thump with which the cat's padded paws used to strike the floor. Half asleep, he switched on the light—and found himself looking into a pair of deadly, staring eyes, set like fatal jewels in a heart-shaped head. Below this he recognized the bloated body of a huge puff adder, some five feet in length and as thick through as a man's leg. In the sudden light, the sooty chevrons and cream-colored crescents blotched with yellow-lake showing on its scaled skin made a blended pattern, like a strip of some malevolent Eastern carpet woven on the loom of death itself.

As the Baas shrank back, there was an intake of whistling breath followed by a fierce hiss as the great snake's swollen body moved itself a foot or so nearer the bed.

The Boer had seen puff adders in action and knew that, in spite of their seeming sluggishness, nothing that lives can surpass in swiftness the flashing stroke of that deadly viper. Bracing his sweating back against the wall, the man waited, holding himself rigidly still. Hissing again, the great serpent pushed forward another foot, and the cruel head raised itself above the bloated coils. At any moment that ghastly demon of the night might start the rush forward, which could end in only one way.

Then, as the Baas clenched his hands so tightly that his nails cut into his wet palms, there came a scratching and a rustle just outside of the window and into the room, with a bound, sprang the lost tiger cat. His sides, which had been so sleek, were sunken, and every rib showed gauntly beneath his silky skin, while bloody welts here and there spoke of the dangers through which he had passed on his long journey home.

Turning like a flash as it felt the vibration of the cat's landing, the great serpent faced the newcomer, hissing horribly. At that breath Lodi crouched, his eyes flamed green-gold in the shadow, and deep in his throat he growled, while his coral gums, curling away from his white, stilettolike teeth, changed his face into a snarling mask of rage, like those lion heads which Assyrian sculptors used to cut in black basalt on the plains of Nineveh six thousand years ago.

For an instant, as cat and snake crouched and coiled, the flaming eyes of the beast met the lidless, dreadful gaze of the serpent. It was Lodi who attacked first. Springing forward, he feinted a lunge with his right forepaw, and, even as he did so, sprang to his left as if shot forward by an uncoiled spring. As he moved, the mouth of the snake opened and from white ridges of gum two crooked, glistening fangs suddenly thrust themselves out from the upper jaw, keener than the sharpest needle ever made by man. As the horrid mouth gaped wide, the inch-long weapons showed tiny openings in their sides, like those in a hypodermic needle, through which the venom would ooze when once their points were sunk deep into the flesh of a victim. Then, just as the cat's body flashed away, with a motion so swift that no human eye could have followed it, the head of the puff adder shot two feet through the air and struck the floor a scant inch from the cat's paw. At the stroke the muscles surrounding the capsule containing the poison ducts contracted and little jets of a limpid yellow liquid bedewed the silken fur of the cat with the very essence of death. Then, like the return of a released spring, the grim head snapped back into the center of the adder's coil once more. Again and again the great cat advanced and retreated, feinting, snarling, springing, until he had provoked the enraged serpent into striking a score of times. Each time only the animal's exquisite sense of distance saved his life, since stroke after stroke of the snake just missed an outstretched paw by a fraction of an inch.

Springing, darting back and forth, and continually circling the bloated body of the huge adder, never once during the first rounds of this duel to the death did the cat sink teeth or claw into its patterned, scaly skin or take chances with the fatal backlash with which a puff adder so often catches an opponent unawares.

At last the snake began to refuse to strike. Still the cat moved around it in swift circles, forcing the adder to move with him in order to keep facing its antagonist.

For some fifteen minutes Lodi feinted and circled, until the puff adder, not built for a long battle, began to move more and more slowly and to show signs of weakness.

At last there came a time when the heavy body was so slow in recoiling that the cat stopped his circling tactics and stared for an instant at the great snake with almost human calculation in his flaming eyes. Then he feinted a last reckless rush, which the viper countered by a lunge which just grazed the cat's outstretched paw. For an instant the fatal head lay flat on the floor. Before it could snap back into place, the cat for the first time struck two lightninglike blows with either paw, ripping his curved black talons through the serpent's skin with a sound like that of tearing silk. Once again the puff adder went back into coil and for the last time struck as the cat plunged in and out. As the serpent lay exhausted, Lodi dabbed at it again with his left forepaw, pinned the deadly head down, and, with a lightninglike spring, drove his four long, fighting teeth through and through the snake's spine and with teeth and claws tore the grinning head clear off from the paralyzed body. Then purring proudly, with arched back, he rubbed his silky side against Baas Vogel's shaking hand.

The Luck of the plantation had come back—and this time to stay!

* * * * *

"Lodi of the Veldt," by Samuel Scoville, Jr. Published in St. Nicholas, *July 1926. Original text owned by Joe Wheeler. Samuel Scoville, Jr. (1872–1950), naturalist and prolific author of books and stories, wrote such books as* Abraham Lincoln, His Story *(1918),* Man and Beast *(1926), and* The Snake Blood Ruby *(1934).*

THE FORCED ARMISTICE

George Inness Hartley

Once before, I'd stumbled on this unforgettable story, read it, then lost track of it. This collection of jungle stories was all but complete, yet gnawing at me night and day was this impulse that refused to go away: Search—no matter how long it takes—until you find that strangest of stories: *two mortal enemies, one a brutal ocelot, and the other a defenseless little monkey who, for a time, forged an almost unbelievable friendship.*

For a time . . .

* * * * *

A shrill, gurgling cry burst from Ot, and he raced for the sanctuary of the higher terraces. From behind came a whining snarl, mingled with the pad of soft feet upon yielding forest mold, causing the half-grown monkey to re-double his efforts. In the palm of Ot's hairy left paw nestled the gray speckled egg that had enticed him so close to the earth, very nearly to his undoing; the other three limbs, together with his slim prehensile tail, served to carry him bounding upward, still gibbering with terror, away from that spotted death that had almost overtaken him. His escape had been accomplished by the merest fraction of a second.

At last the fleeing monkey halted, with a grunt of relief, among the upper reaches and settled himself comfortably athwart a spreading bed of twigs. The risk had been great, but the reward even greater. His eyes glistened and the miraculously preserved egg vanished between his jaws, causing his lips to droop from the ecstasy of that wonderful flavor, while the rich fluid trickled slowly down his throat. The heavenly operation completed, he gazed down upon the baffled ocelot, who returned his look with such a vindictive glare that Ot, in spite of his position of safety, gave a gasp of apprehension. Then he laughed at his fears and made a taunting gesture at the beast. The cat retorted with a spiteful growl, but Ot only jeered the louder, imitating that disappointed snarl and deriding the creature's helplessness. Then, tiring of the game, he sped to the tip of the purple heart tree, where he could have a clearer view of the surrounding jungle. The cat sprang into a dense labyrinth of twisted lianas and there crouched, vowing vengeance.

A hundred feet beneath Ot flowed a river, a broad, chocolate-hued torrent that roared with savage impressiveness between sheer jungle walls. The stream was an evil thing, a meeting place of jagged rocks that projected everywhere throughout its bed, growling rapids of creamy foam, swirling eddies, dangerous falls, and unceasing thunder, menacing and racking, of pent-up waters that grappled and fought for outlet to the broader, deeper reaches farther on. It inspired one with awe.

But the monkey wasted little thought upon the rush and bluster of this river; such unfettered turbulence was too old a story to awaken any untoward excitement in his breast. His quick eyes had fastened upon a brilliant patch of crimson, gleaming from the border of a swaying mat of vines that dangled from a lower branch of a neighboring tree. The water meant nothing, the vivid patch everything. That burning red spot against the background of green spelt food, delicious food, the most appetizing viand of all—a cluster of rich, ripe, luscious figs. And half-grown Ot was always hungry.

The youngster uttered a grunt of complete satisfaction. Without a second glance at the brawling cataract, he scrambled to the outer curtain of foliage, which overhung the rapids, and in less time than it takes to tell, he had traversed half the distance toward his goal. Then a short leap brought him to a looped vine to which he clung while this "monkey ladder" waved dizzily back and forth, not forty feet above the booming torrent.

Far from being frightened, Ot enjoyed his wild ride. The ocelot had been forgotten; this was life! Having obtained a firm hold with his tail upon the liana, he howled and jabbered at the furious water—which now for the first time he seemed to note—made disrespectful motions with his hands, grinned contemptuously, and in every way declared his scorn for the sputtering whirlpool that could not get at him. He even attempted to set up a rival roar that would drown out its angry mutterings; but his voice cracked, and he broke off in confusion for fear old Ap, the most accomplished howler of the troupe, might overhear and laugh. Then, at last tiring of his useless defiance, which met with small notice from below, he hastened toward the awaiting fruit cluster.

It would have been well for the monkey had he examined this particular tangle, with some of his usual acuteness, before commencing the feast. But the lesson received from his nest-robbing adventure had already slipped from his memory. And after his unanswered defiance to the river, he felt unusually brave and reckless. He craved food—a continual state of his; therefore caution was abandoned, and he snatched at a handful of bleeding figs. Other handfuls followed in rapid succession until through sheer lack of breath he was forced to pause. He had been famished. He reached for more.

Just at that moment a rustle in the entanglement close to his elbow caused him to desist, with arm half extended toward the figs. He cast a suspicious glance around. A stealthy undulation of branches, a faint, almost unnoticeable swaying, centered his attention upon an enormous air plant that had spread its wide, tobaccolike fronds from a mass of rotting twigs a few feet above him. Those shining leaves quivered, gently, almost imperceptibly, yet he was certain that they moved. Yes, and a bit of tawny yellow showed behind them, tawny spotted with black. It, too, moved!

Ot stiffened with alarm. His heart sank, then bounded into his throat. He gasped. Summoning his scattered wits, he attempted to back cautiously off to a point where he could make a dash for liberty; but he found that he could not for the despised river lay behind him. It was impossible to drop down through the vines, because these overlooked the current; to return by the path he had come was to pass close to that spreading plant and the hideous thing it screened. Too late, Ot realized that he had been careless; now he was cornered and in desperate straits. From behind that wide-leafed epiphyte, death stared him in the face, a fiend lurked there who owned two malignant, yellow eyes, agleam with triumph, which at that very moment were boring straight into his own and freezing him. And the river laughed from below, a malicious, haunting laugh that Ot had suddenly grown to hate.

The owner of the ferocious orbs lashed his tail in a frenzy of consuming desire. His slim lithe form had flattened upon a bed of leaves, and his muscles steadily tightened for the spring that was to bring down his prey. For he, too, like Ot, was hungry; and a half-grown howler was the choicest of all morsels for a famished ocelot, especially a howler that had recently ridiculed him. With the utmost patience he had stalked his victim, moving only when the monkey moved, creeping stealthily inch by inch, gaining a foot each time he groped for more figs, biding his time, always soundless, patient, wary, and revengeful; and now he had at last drawn within striking distance. His eyes sparkled with joy, his long tail pulsed like the quivering of a bushmaster's spike; even the vivid black spots upon his back seemed to glow with ferocity and bloodthirst. He was ready.

All hope had fled from Ot. Every avenue of escape was closed to him. Now his limbs seemed divorced from his body, utterly refusing to answer the shout from his brain that he must flee or die. Just barely was he able to cling to the vines. And then, when at last that hulking thing flashed from its hiding place, bore gloatingly down upon him, his nerveless grip entirely relaxed. He was going. This was the end!

Providence, perhaps, proved kinder to the unfortunate monkey than he deserved for his recent negligence. The ocelot sprang, but too late; his victim was gone, vanished from his sight. As his grip had loosened from the vine, Ot had toppled over backward. For a full second he sprawled downward, then with a wail of despair, plunged head first into the boiling river. The cat, disconcerted by the sudden disappearance of the prize which he already deemed his, landed awkwardly upon the vine, failed to recover his balance, and before he quite realized what had happened, slid spitting and squawling after the monkey.

The terrified Ot came to the surface, some fifty feet beyond the point where he had entered the water. Unaware of what he did, obeying his first impulse, he struck manfully out for the fast receding bank. Although this was the first time the monkey had ever been immersed, he nevertheless swam with the ease of an accomplished swimmer, employing a strong paddle stroke, wholly a gift from instinct. Had he fallen other than into the heart of a rushing torrent, he would have quickly attained a point of safety; but now in that hurly-burly wash he became a plaything, a speck of living flotsam to be tossed at will. The river, too, was having its revenge for insult.

But Ot was no longer willing to die without a struggle. He fought bravely to reach a low-hanging liana, of which great numbers whipped at the foam close by; but the effort proved unavailing, except to exhaust his strength. Slowly, with cruel persistence, the laughing current dragged him away from the bank. An unexpected eddy sucked at his body, drew him under, and spewed him up, more than half-drowned, a hundred feet further on. Blinded by flying spray, he maintained the unequal struggle. His fingers encountered the sharp edge of a rock, and he swung partly free of the water.

The rock proved only a temporary relief. A foaming surge loosened his hold, snatched him up, and hurled his battered form down a ten-foot drop in the streambed. He struck heavily against an outstanding boulder, so hard that what little breath remained to him was forcibly expelled from his body. Choking and half dead, he flung out his arms. They encountered a large, floating object upon which, with great difficulty, he managed to drag himself. Then flat on his stomach and quite unconscious, he went spinning down the churning current on his unknown craft.

The little monkey awakened in a daze, as though he had just emerged from a harrowing dream. He felt weak and thoroughly nauseated. His teeth chattered with cold; he was chilled to the marrow. All sensation had gone from his thin, whiplike tail; that necessary appendage hung heavy and numb and useless. His vitality had sunk to a low ebb.

Presently, by dint of forced effort, Ot lifted his head to take in his surroundings. What he saw brought a feeble, half-hopeful grunt from his parted lips. A trembling hand swept his face and he blinked as though dazzled by the sight. Instead of the partly submerged log on which he had thought himself, his eyes encountered nothing but green leaves, with a tag of blue sky gleaming through here and there. Rising upon his hands, with renewed vigor, he discerned tall limbs towering overhead, twisted and warped as though from the battering of a gale, yet real branches and a true treetop! He uttered a sigh of relief and then, feeling uncommonly tired, fell into a doze.

The monkey did not sleep long. A few minutes after closing his eyes, his body fell such a prey to chills that he was compelled to cling with all the strength he could muster to a twig to save himself from a sudden drop. How cold he felt! He glanced downward and almost lost his grip. A moan of despair burst from him. Water, horrible water, flowed there, not six inches below; his tail had been dragging in it! It was a treetop, to be sure, to which he clung, but the tree had sunk deep in the river and was adrift.

Presently, regaining a tiny atom of courage, he gingerly parted the leaves to one side. Now his worst fears were confirmed. A wide expanse of water, smooth, unmarred by a single ripple, shone there; and a mile distant lay a blue-and-yellow barrier, the jungle that had been his home. He was marooned!

The distressed youngster broke down. He was lost, stranded, helpless, sick. He could not swim that intervening mile, would not have attempted it even if the distance had been but fifty feet, for he feared and hated the touch of water and only navigated it through instinct. Fainting and utterly wretched, he felt ready to die.

But the sun, boring down with all its tropical warmth, soon began to infuse a little fire into his veins. His auburn hair lost its dull, sodden appearance, softened, and began to gleam again in all its old-time glory. The numbness in his tail departed; that member throbbed with pain for a while, and then regained its former virility. The hold of his fingers upon the smaller branches tightened, grew more assured, firmer. His nausea left him. He felt better.

However, despite the increase of bodily comfort, Ot's courage failed to mount in proportion. Stark dread blanketed his mind and weighed his spirits down. Nervous and ill at ease, he wedged himself into a fork and there, with lackluster eyes, watched the river ripple slowly past his floating prison. He detested that gentle gurgle now, hated it more than he had hated anything else in his life—even the jungle cats—for it seemed to mock him, to chuckle over his helplessness, in much the same way that he had jeered at the boiling rapids back there in the hills when he was safely astride his "monkey ladder." And now he vowed that until his leafy raft grounded against the far-off forest wall or—fearful thought!—sank from beneath him, he would not leave his present perch, come what might. He had not the energy or the desire to move.

While he thus mournfully cogitated, a new sound, a sort of sibilant sigh, caused the castaway to glance at a big limb running parallel to his, some two yards distant. The object that met his eyes drew from him a broken, gasping shudder. He uttered a single horrified moan, then forgetting the recent promise to himself, sprang for the highest tip of the tree. The ocelot, that same hideous, sneaking beast that had brought him to this pass, was a fellow passenger. They were afloat together!

Ot charged, panic-stricken, to the thinnest shoot that would bear his weight and there clung for several minutes, teetering frantically back and forth, prey to untold terror. At length, seeing that the beast made no move to approach, he warily descended to a firmer seat, where a single bound could carry him back to the precarious safety of the twig-end. But the ocelot remained tightly wedged, just as Ot had been, in a sloping crotch; and not by so much as a flicker of an eyelid did he seem to be aware of the presence of the monkey. His attention centered solely upon the brown eddies that swept past, and his attitude was one of blank, profound despair.

Ot would not have been a true monkey had not his curiosity at last forced discretion into the background. Timidly at first, then with more assurance, he lowered himself toward the brooding cat. Only when five feet separated them did he halt, prepared for a hasty retirement, if the occasion arose. But still the ocelot did not move. Gaining courage, Ot grunted. The cat slowly raised his head.

This action on the part of his enemy was more than the monkey could stand. Upon the instant all his freshly acquired bravery oozed away, and he leapt for the top of the tree, jabbering hysterically. The eyes of the cat returned to the water. With his panic somewhat abated, Ot once more descended, and again he grunted. As before, the ocelot lifted his head in response, and Ot had much ado to keep from bolting. But this time he maintained a firmer grip upon himself; he gurgled a humble greeting. The fierce, yellow orbs met his, and Ot started, but did not flee. The eyes were soft and friendly and sad now; they spoke of no glowering hatred, only subdued humility. And when he grunted a third time, the cat did not growl; he looked glad and purred.

And so that ill-chosen pair, one a flinty-hearted killer, the other at worst a harmless boaster, found companionship on that unlucky voyage. Irony of fate and fear of swirling waters made them comrades in adversity, and each discovered consolation in the presence of the other.

The tree continued its slow journey before the current, bearing its strange freight. Hours slipped by. Self-possession had largely returned to the monkey, and he exercised by exploring each leaf and branch upon the tree. The ocelot still remained in his fork, but whenever Ot drew near, he greeted him with a pleasant, purring sound or a soft, tremulous sigh. Once he made a playful pass with his paw, with nails sheathed, but Ot darted out of reach with a friendly chuckle. Even though Ot no longer feared the killer, he had no desire to become too intimate. The action had been due to no evil intent on the ocelot's part, merely an expression of thanks for Ot's presence there, as he well knew; but thereafter he performed his antics at a safer distance.

A breeze sprang up from the north, the daily offspring of the Caribbean trades, and beat the river surface into a multitude of frothy waves. Later it increased to half a gale, causing the top-heavy tree to cant dangerously from side to side. In one of these sudden shifts, Ot was caught quite unprepared and hurled into the river. A few strokes served to carry him back to the tree, to the point where the ocelot crouched, and, by climbing directly across his body, Ot found a perch a few feet above the cat. Subdued and crestfallen by his renewed wetting, he remained there.

The uncomfortable tilting of the tree increased. At times its two occupants expected it to roll over, dousing and, perhaps, drowning the pair of them, so violent had grown the waves and so strong the wind. Each lurch and sudden plunge elicited a despairing wail from the monkey; the cat sobbed in terror. Both clung to their branches not two feet apart.

But the wind, though it threatened their destruction, at the same time served to drive their wallowing craft toward shore. Hardly an hour had elapsed since the first rocking gust when Ot, glancing dolefully landward, was electrified to see the jungle wall scarcely a hundred yards off. Unable to believe the evidence of his senses, he rubbed his eyes and stared again. It was true. Land now lay very near. An excited cough from his companion showed that he, too, had glimpsed it, and had aroused from his lethargic state.

And so the jungle cat and the monkey, gripping tight to their vibrating supports, viewed the nearing of the trees. Their bodies shook with the intensity of their eagerness, with their joy at the idea of escape. Drawn by this great common desire, they crept closer together, until their hairy forms pressed one against the other; and thus they clung, with eyes only for that garlanded mass that they approached so slowly.

Then while yet a hundred feet from the bank, their swaying craft grounded. For a sickening instant it hung there, then slid partly over, and once more floated. Inch by inch it drifted in toward the trees, hesitated several times upon the muddy shallows, then touched the outer fringe and stuck. A broad, horizontal limb, projecting far out over the river, struck through the foliage straight to the very base of the fork which now housed the two castaways, and formed a bridge that pointed inland to home and food and safety. The voyage was done.

For half a minute these two creatures of the forest sat crouching side by side with fur rubbing against fur, each utterly blind to the presence of the other, both consumed by the delight of their homecoming. Ot was the first to emerge from his stupor. A strange, wild look entered his eyes. Darting a suspicious glance at his close companion, he gave birth to a startled squeal and leaped for the waiting bridge. A second later he had gained the trunk of a great mora to which the saving limb belonged. There, gripping hard at a thick vine partly coiled about the trunk, he turned a frightened face, all twitching with fear, toward the ocelot.

That tawny creature, Ot's erstwhile friend, now crept stealthily toward the monkey along the bridge. The eyes of the cat no longer shone with soft, sympathetic light or with humility; they glittered with all their ancient fire, breathing hatred and death. His tail lashed savagely at the leaves, and he had flattened as though about to spring.

Ot gave one little shriek of terror. With a desperate upward bound, he clutched at the shaggy bark of the encircling liana. Like a flash of golden sun ray he scrambled up the trunk, then out upon a twisted branch that interlocked with a neighboring tree. There safe and free, he tarried to look down.

The disappointed cat still clung to the bridging bough, glaring up at the monkey with an expression of terrible anger. The armistice was at an end.

* * * * *

"The Forced Armistice," by George Inness Hartley. Published in St. Nicholas, *August 1927. Original text owned by Joe Wheeler. George Inness Hartley, born in 1887, besides writing many stories for popular magazines during the first half of the twentieth century, also wrote books such as* The Last Parakeet *(1923) and* The Lost Flamingo *(1924).*

The Ambulance of Aldabra

Frank Mallow

Ambulances come in many shapes and sizes—but who'd have imagined one like this! This story took place in 1917.

* * * * *

On a morning in November seven years ago, the bark *Deborah Dulk,* of Port Townsend, put into the sequestered harborage of Tatat, one of the un-inhabited islets of the Aldabra group in the Indian Ocean. The forest of Tatat affords excellent firewood, and pure fresh water is to be had from a copious spring convenient to the anchorage. For these good reasons, the little island was a favorite rendezvous for whaling vessels as long as two generations ago, when whale-fishing was a highly important business of the sea and American sailing ships excelled all others in the enterprise and daring with which they pursued that adventurous calling.

Captain Abram Dulk had been a whaler in his youth, and in his hardy old age, being master of his own ship, not infrequently humored a yearning to revisit some haunt of his adventurous prime. This was his real reason for touching at Tatat, but his supposed purpose was to take on fresh water.

About three o'clock in the afternoon of the day the bark arrived, three

members of her crew on shore leave were leisurely finding their way through the not difficult jungle that covers the islet. Though dense enough to shut out the direct rays of the sun, the forest was not gloomy, but rather suffused with soft light. The island was ringed with coconut palms; but inland the tapering toon and the slender ironwood trees predominated. There were others equally graceful, with feathery or fronded tops outspread like lace-trimmed parasols. Brilliant-hued birds-of-paradise and other beautiful winged creatures were numerous, as well as many small, quaint animals. But nowhere did the sailors discover evidence of human presence or passage.

When, therefore, they came upon a wide, deep-worn trail through the primitive woodland, it became at once the object of their keen curiosity. The strange path averaged several feet wide and was worn down to bed gravel. At first glance, one assumed it to have been washed out by the heavy tropical rains common to the region; but this was disproved by the fact that it followed the undulations of the ground, so that in places the water would have run off, since it would not run uphill.

"It's a porpoise portage," declared Carpenter Andy Gluart, called Chips by his shipmates, as are all ship's carpenters.

"What's a porpoise portage?" unthinkingly inquired Harry Firman, known as Beastie among his friends, because that was what he called all animals and birds.

Firman was an apprentice, sixteen years old, in training to be a ship's officer. Unlike old Andy, who was a loquacious jester, Harry was frugal of speech. His seeming reserve was due largely to the preoccupation of a studious mind. If Harry had enjoyed better educational advantages, he would probably have been planning to be a college professor or perhaps an exploring naturalist. His favorite recreation was the study of animals and their ways, both domestic and wild, and he was much given to making pets of the former. It was characteristic of him that though he was an acknowledged marksman of merit and always carried a revolver in his belt on expeditions of this kind, he was never known to shoot a wild creature.

Chips was denied a chance to explain what he meant by a porpoise portage. His explanation would have been a mere sailor's yarn, anyway, in the spinning of which he delighted. His first sentence was cut short by a yell from Mike O'Hannon, the third member of the party. Mike whirled about with a loud outcry and started on the backtrack with such haste and disregard of obstructions that he got his feet tangled in ground vines and fell sprawling. The two others backed away from the path in indecisive alarm.

"Look out, boys!" warned O'Hannon. "There's a snake as big as a scuttlebutt coming down that trail. It has a head as big as yours, Beastie."

At this announcement, the others retired with scarcely less promptitude than had Mike himself. Concealed in the foliage at a discreet distance from the path, the three held a debate and endeavored to discover the enemy. It developed that O'Hannon had noted nothing of the monster but its head, and his description of that was obviously exaggerated. Curiosity curbing fear, the seamen stealthily approached the trail again.

The situation was relieved by Andy when he finally caught a glimpse of the unknown terror. He had been well frightened and quite at a loss; but now he assumed a pose of pretended courage and wisdom.

"Hun—sarpint!" he scoffed. "Mebby you think the great sea-sarpint is on shore leave."

"Likely as porpoises," retorted Mike. "What is it? Do you see it?"

"Come on! It's only a joint torkus." Chips boldly stepped back into the trail.

There was no denying that the veteran ship's carpenter, who had spent the greater part of his life seafaring under Captain Dulk, had firsthand knowledge of many things strange to his younger companions. They followed him now with confidence. "Joint torkus" proved to be his pronunciation of "giant tortoise," and certainly the designation well fitted the creature creeping down the jungle path. It appeared to be a little less than five feet long by fully three wide, and its high, rounded shell gave it added magnitude. The only repulsive thing about the creature was its head, which was set on an elongated neck, and which, seen alone, might well cause it to be mistaken for a monster serpent.

Mike and Beastie had seen sea turtles of remarkable size in the lagoons of Mexico and other places. But this was a land tortoise and larger than any turtle either of them had ever seen—much larger. Andy's lips smacked with audible relish of the lecture in natural history that he could now deliver to his shipmates, and without indulging in exaggeration.

"There ain't but one other place on yearth," he said, "where you could find a joint torkus as big as this one. That's in the Galapagos Islands. I seed one there fight a dog, and the dog had the worst of it. It got too near the torkus's head. That torkus can stretch its neck and throw its head about like throwin' out a moorin' line. A torkus ain't a turkle [turtle]. A turkle lives in the water and a torkus lives on land. But there ain't no turkles get as big as torkuses do. A torkus is too slow to round up on you or chase you, so they ain't dangerous except you get too close to their heads. This trail was made by this here torkus and a lot more like him. You follow this trail and it'll take you to fresh water—a spring of it. And you'll find a whole school of torkuses there drinkin' together, just as sociable as folks. That's what this old feller is after—water; and nothin' won't stop him gettin' it short of hittin' him in the head. You could ride on his back and he wouldn't care a mite. Looky!"

He stepped onto the back of the tortoise and balanced himself there with extended arms. The cumbrous steed gave no sign.

The congregating of the tortoises at a drinking pool was one statement made by Andy which was susceptible of being verified or disproved. It was like Beastie Firman that he should at once resolve to see for himself. Andy and Mike, bent on visiting the opposite side of the island, tried in vain to dissuade him. So the party divided, Harry following the trail.

He soon overtook a second tortoise traveling in the same direction as the first, and with the same patient slowness. Soon after passing around it, his attention was attracted by a small animal in a tree, which he took to be a diminutive monkey. But its gray coat and long muzzle, the latter revealed as it peered down from the lofty limb along which it lay stretched, were unlike those of any monkey he had ever seen. It resembled a North American opossum and acted like a South American sloth. It did not seem to be disturbed when he threw sticks at it, though, to be sure, these fell far short of the high branch to which the odd creature clung.

Beastie could not bring himself to pass by a strange animal without trying to identify its species. The towering tree, without a limb for more than forty feet, was an easy climb to a sailor. Before leaving the ship, he had prepared himself for scaling coconut trees by the simple expedient of doubling the length of his belt. This he did by buckling two belts together, end to end. He now let this out so that it loosely enclosed both himself and the tree trunk, and, by pressing his knees against the latter, he was able to support himself with slight effort and to ascend with ease, having merely to steady himself with his hands.

He quickly climbed within reach of the lowest branch, which seemed perfectly sound, and took hold of it to draw himself up. But it proved his undoing, for, evidently decayed, it broke in his grasp. When reaching upward, it had been necessary to allow his belt, till then kept taut by leaning back in it, to slacken, and to depend on the bough to bear his weight. Thus left for the moment without any support, he slipped through the leather ring, and fell to the ground.

He turned completely over in his descent, striking the ground feet first, but with his legs drawn up. These acted as a spring to save the rest of his body from injury; but his left leg, which bore the brunt of the shock, was broken and partly crushed by contact with an imbedded rock. The wrench and pain were so severe that for a time the boy was unaware of a fracture of his right ankle.

When he was able to take stock of his injuries, he realized that he was helpless. He had landed on the edge of the tortoise trail and continued to lie there, his head and shoulders in the path, his body hidden among some giant ferns. An attempt to move only wrung from him a low cry of pain, quickly suppressed. He uttered no other sound except to send up a few feeble halloos for help. Then he fired his revolver, until only a few shells were left. These he kept for possible need should he have to defend himself from wild creatures of the jungle. The bark was, he knew, about a mile to the south. He could not hope that his shipmates there would hear his cries, and his late companions ashore were doubtless out of earshot. Nor was it at all likely that any attention would be paid to the sound of shots, as Andy and Mike also carried firearms and would probably be shooting for sport, while the latter would think he was doing the same. Harry's predicament was grave. It was not likely that he would be sought for before nightfall, and in the meantime he would suffer greatly.

The thirst that always accompanies great physical pain soon assailed him. The small creatures of the woods began moving around him, unafraid, since he did not molest them or make any motion. Parrots and other birds of gorgeous plumage chattered and fluttered almost within his reach. He saw a giant tortoise coming down the trail, no doubt the one he had so lately passed by. He remembered that this tortoise was on its way to water. A few minutes before he had smiled at its slow advance toward a thing desired. He wished now that he could travel as fast and painlessly as it did. Because it was bound for water, and because that was the thing that he himself wanted just then more than anything else in the world, his eyes and mind remained on the clodlike creature, creeping on so slowly but surely. Brother to the clod it might be, but it had intelligence and a will and a way to seek the satisfaction of its want.

The few minutes that the tortoise took to come abreast of him seemed interminable. The dangerous-looking head at last drew even with his own, not more than three feet away; but it did not threaten him and he did not fear it. He seemed incapable of any coherent thought except that the tortoise would lead him to water if only he could follow it. It was slowly passing him by, would soon be gone. The near edge of the shell, a great, roughly saw-toothed curve, brushed his sleeve. He lifted the arm on high to keep it clear, and then involuntarily, he knew not why, let it fall again, his fingers just topping the crest, his arm resting across the slope of the corrugated mound. Instinctively, he clutched the ragged ridge over which his fingers hung. He closed his eyes in the way that suffering persons do when undertaking movement, as if that might blot out the pain of exertion.

Slowly, steadily, with such height of resolution as comes only to one striving for his life, he drew himself upward.

Overcome by his effort, Harry swooned away, and lay inert for a brief period, his outstretched figure bent over the curve of the creature's back. But due to the gentle, almost imperceptible motion of the tortoise, its living, but helpless, burden was not dislodged. Harry's last clear recollection was of himself calling for water, though fully conscious that nobody was near to give it to him.

About the time that Harry had separated from his companions in the forest, a party of men from the *Deborah Dulk*, detailed to take on fresh water, were floating their casks ashore. The casks, lashed together into a raft, were anchored, bungs up, within wading distance of the beach sands. An advance guard of two men had already penetrated the woods, here sparse and bouldery, toward a spot at which Mate Hovey had told them that they would find a spring of pure, sweet water emptying from a crevice in the rocks into an overflowing pool. The two soon returned to the beach with an exciting yarn.

The spring and pool were, they said, in possession of a school of turtles as big as the midship deck house. Mr. Hovey brusquely directed them to return, drive off the turtles, and get the water, concluding his order with an admonition familiar to all sailors.

"No matter how you do it—do it!" he said.

The whole party had a hilarious time trying to obey that order. The part of it relating to routing the turtles proved impracticable. Tortoises cannot, they found, be shooed like chickens nor scatted like cats. So they began filling and carrying buckets with a discreet watch on the homely heads and sharp little eyes all around them. There were turtles (as the deep-water men persisted in calling them) occasionally arriving and others departing. Soon little attention was being paid them. Dean Hance, an ordinary seaman, who answered to the nickname of Thrifty, alone maintained an unabated interest.

"There comes another," he announced after awhile. "Look—it's got a double hump!"

The latest comer, a short distance up the trail, appeared, in truth, malformed, a shapeless ridge being discernible across its back.

"Say!" exclaimed Thrifty, again. "That one's hollerin'. Listen—hear him bellow!"

A hoarse, low cry, coming from the direction of the approaching tortoise, caused all hands to stop work and look up, regarding one another with questioning eyes.

"It's hollerin' for water," interpreted Thrifty. "Hear it? It says 'water' plain. I'm goin' to find out about this."

He made off up the trail, detouring a little to avoid directly encountering the tortoise, beside which he stopped and stood staring in amazement.

"I say, fellows, come here!" he shrilled. "Come quick! Come here, men!"

A few minutes later, still bearing the stricken sailor on its back, a giant tortoise drew up beside the forest pool and imperturbably craned its long neck in the act of drinking. Already the cruel thirst in Firman's throat had been allayed by copious draughts of the cool water which willing hands had hurriedly brought in response to his entreaties. And then as many of the men as could crowded forwarded and tenderly lifted their helpless shipmate from the strangest and strongest, if perhaps slowest, ambulance that ever brought a human wreck into safe harbor.

* * * * *

"The Ambulance of Aldabra," by Frank Mallow. Published in St. Nicholas, *January 1924. Original text owned by Joe Wheeler. Frank Mallow wrote for popular magazines during the first half of the twentieth century.*

BIG ROO

Vance Joseph Hoyt

The little kangaroo unknowingly had grown to his life's most dangerous stage: too large to safely hide in his mother's pouch and too weak to keep up with the big roos when fleeing from predators.

Now a pack was closing in on him—was all lost?

* * * * *

Deep in the bush of faraway Australia, several doe kangaroos and their fat young moved leisurely through the night down a grass-fringed path to the shore of a small artificial lake. Joey was the larger of the little leapers and just one year of age. He felt bold and very important as he bounded along at his mother's side on his hoppers. Now and then he paused, balanced on the arch of his tail and looked at the big world about him.

For a moment he thus posed, his extremely short forearms drooped like the paws of a begging dog, his tall, erect ears straining for the least sound, and his dewy soft eyes staring with glowing wonder. It was a beautiful world that he observed, and the sight of it thrilled him with joy.

Chut! Chut! Chut-ch-ch-ch-ch! He hopped after his mother, the mouse-colored fur of his body a robe of exquisite beauty in the soft moonlight.

Joey had seen his father, Big Roo, but once in his lifetime, a giant kangaroo who weighed nearly three hundred pounds and towered more than seven feet when he stood upright upon toes and great tail. He was known among the few settlers as the "old man of the bush," and he could race with the speed of the wind, thirty feet to the bound.

Someday Joey himself would be a masterful monarch of his own domain. But of such things the small kangaroo could not now possibly know. Unmindful of the many dangers of fang and claw that ever lurked in the offing, he and the other little kangaroos played tag on the grassy slope of the lake, clutching at one another with their tiny hands as their mothers fended in the lush lily patch at the water's edge.

They chirruped and hopped about in the near vicinity of their parents, each striving to pounce upon the other's tail in leaps of hilarity. The does in the green-picking seemingly paid little attention to the frolicking young. Yet, the soft glow of the moon revealed that the large deerlike eyes of one of them were constantly upon the little leapers, or probing the surrounding dark shadows for the least sign of an enemy.

From all visible appearances the scene was one of a happy kangaroo gathering enjoying the evening meal and play with never a thought of danger. Still, there was the feeling of tenseness that held every creature aquiver for instant flight if need be.

A tiny rustle in the deep grass up the slope instantly froze every doe erect on her great tail, back bowed rearward, tall ears flickering, sensitive as microphones. Likewise, the joeys ceased with their play and stood alert, like little soldiers, peering cautiously into the night.

There was a movement, ever so slight, and for a flash, two points of light glittered in the tall grass, green and menacing. The sharp eyes of the does, fashioned for darkness, were quick to catch the shaggy but wolflike body of a dingo, the wild dog of Australia and terror of all the kangaroo people.

The movement broke the suspense, and adult and young alike sprang in all directions. Mothers scooped their little ones into their pouches and boxed larger babies into bouncing flight.

Joey saw the sinister form of their greatest enemy bearing down upon them. He chirruped with fright and bounded toward his mother, who had leaped out of the water in his direction. Springing into the air, he turned a somersault in an attempt to land in her pouch. But the next instant, Joey fell upon the ground, all fours in the air.

Hitherto, he had always been swished away in his mother's furry cradle to speedy safety. Quickly he regained his legs and again somersaulted into the air. And once more he landed upon the ground. He had suddenly grown too large to enter his mother's pouch. Then Warragal, the black leader of the dingo pack, was upon them.

Chirruping frantically for her son to flee for his life, Joey's mother struck at the wild dog with her powerful hind hocks; leaped into the air, flaying with her muscular tail as if it were a cudgel. But the doe was no match for the dingo.

Joey twittered in rage and hopped around in circles, not knowing what to do. He did not want to leave his mother, and because he was too inexperienced to realize the danger that threatened him, he refused to follow in the flight of the other does and joeys.

Then, to Joey, the whole world suddenly seemed filled with flying bodies. A great gray form came bounding through the tall grass down the slope toward the lake, and in a single leap, nearly forty feet away, landed upon the savage wild dog in a whirlwind of flaying hoppers.

It was Big Roo, Joey's father; he had come to the rescue of the doe and his offspring. Delivering blows with his rear legs that were as powerful as the kick of an ostrich, the giant kangaroo hurled the wild dog far out into the lake.

Striking the water in a howling splash, Warragal turned tail and swam to the opposite shore, where he slunk up the bank, decidedly worse for the fray but far from being conquered. Sitting on his haunches, he yapped long and loudly. In the distance answered his pack. Nearer and nearer his followers drew, called to the death chase.

Quickly sensing a greater danger, the old boomer nudged his mate and Joey, speaking to them in the silent language of the wild that they must be gone. Without pausing longer, the three bounded up the slope through the tall grass and vanished over a low rising.

For some time Big Roo led his family deeper into the bush. When single, or even in pairs, he did not fear the wild dogs. He could easily outwit the combined efforts of any three of them. But when in pack, it would be impossible for him to protect the doe and Joey from so many fangs. By all means he must prevent such a clash—if possible.

The doe was only slightly hurt from the conflict; it was no trouble for her to keep up with her mate. But Joey experienced considerable difficulty in maintaining the speed of his parents. Because of the shortness of his legs he had to hop several times as often as the older ones. He was quickly growing weary, and as he fell behind, he began to complain.

"*Chut! Chut! Chut-ch-ch-ch!*" he called for his mother to wait for him, fearful lest he should be left to the mercy of the great danger from which they were fleeing.

"*Chut! Ch-ch!*" his mother answered and waited for Joey to come abreast, when she touched him affectionately with her nose and nudged him on to greater speed. But Joey was unable to keep up with the pace of his father and mother.

Several times the doe tried to assist him into her pouch, but to no avail. Then, in her desperation, she stayed by his side and waited for the little leaper to rest his tired hoppers. Her large sad eyes shone fearfully in the moonlight as she looked back through the bush in the direction from which came the howling of the dingoes.

Uttering a strange sound that Joey had never heard before, Big Roo came bounding back to them. For a long moment he stood at his full height, staring with great luminous eyes in the direction of the lake. Again that strange sound twittered in his deep throat, a sound that set every hair of Joey's body on end.

The next instant, "the old man of the bush" bounced away a short distance and leaped upon a huge pile of rocks. Then he reared, a majestic figure in the night, to better view the approach of their enemies. Over the top of the mallee scrub forest, Warragal and his pack of six dingoes could be seen in the moonlight, drifting across a small clearing, hot upon their trail.

Leaping down from the mass of rocks, Big Roo bounded back to the doe and the little leaper. Of course there was no way that Joey and his mother could tell what the giant kangaroo had seen. From his actions, however, their infallible senses told them all that they needed to know—the pack was speedily bringing their flight to a close.

Nuzzling Joey along the jowls, the doe bounded on after Big Roo, eager for the safety of her young. Chirruping excitedly, the little leaper got to his hoppers and followed. Still, no matter how hard he tried, he lagged behind.

Finally, the crafty old kangaroo led the doe and his joey into a dense thicket and bedded them there. Then leaping along the trail they had left in the bush, for a quarter of a mile or more, he paused on a small knoll. Here he raised to full height, plainly silhouetted in the moonlight, and stood boldly observing the wild dogs sweeping up the slope toward him.

For a tense moment he waited until the black leader was almost upon him; so close that he was seen by every member of the pack. And this is the very thing that Big Roo had hoped would happen. With a shrill whistle of rage, he bounded off at right angles to the thread of his back trail, carrying the dingoes with him, close upon his every leap. The chase was on!

Hurdling the landscape, the giant kangaroo fairly took wing, his four-toed hoppers and mighty tail scarcely touching the earth. His short forearms were drooped upon his chest, his slender neck and head stretched out, and his long rabbitlike ears were laid back, vibrant to the swish of the whispering wind. Of all the wild joys, to race before a pack of dingoes was the thing Big Roo loved best.

Farther and farther he led his enemies from the hiding place of the doe and the little leaper. But the speed at which he was forced to travel made the feat a hazardous one. The distance of every leap had to be gauged to the fraction of an inch. The least error might send him tumbling headlong to break his neck or be rended by the terrible fangs of Warragal and his followers before he could regain his hoppers.

Especially was he careful on down slopes, where it was difficult to maintain his balance against the momentum of his flight. Such places he shunned as much as possible, preferring the rise of the land where it was easier to outdistance the pack. In particular he sought the scrub forest where he could clear the dense shrubbery in mighty bounds, while the dingoes were forced to struggle through brier and bramble at a great disadvantage.

Coming to a narrow stream of water, he leaped to the opposite bank and bounded up the slope over the rise out of sight. The dingoes plunged into the water and swam furiously, losing precious ground. In a few moments, however, they, too, vanished over the knoll, gaining on their prey.

Big Roo had never been in this part of the country before. He suddenly found himself in a parklike plain which was not to his liking. In the open, the pack could quickly overtake him, or he would be winded at the speed he was traveling. Now that the doe and the little leaper were safe, he must deal with his enemies forthwith.

Scanning the moonlit plain for some haven to his advantage, his keen eyes fell upon a distant clump of trees. He immediately veered toward them, lengthening his bounds as he did so. But even as he reached the eucalypti, the black leader was close upon him. Whirling and leaning his back against the trunk of a great eucalyptus, Big Roo took a stand.

Far in advance of his followers, Warragal, the terror of the bush, sprang straight for the throat of his quarry. But the thing that met his rush was the reaping-hook toe of the giant kangaroo's mighty right hopper. Catapulting through the air, the black leader landed twenty feet away in the path of the oncoming pack.

Pausing only for an instant to view the still form of his greatest enemy, Big Roo leaped away, thirty feet to the lunge. Several of the pack followed him, but he soon left them hopelessly in the rear.

Bounding into a savanna of tall kangaroo grass, Big Roo hopped on and on, circling in the direction of the small lake.

The full moon was sinking low in the western sky when he came thumping down the long slope to the water's edge. The scent of lilies filled his nostrils and a low, questioning chirruping broke the deep silence. The doe had returned to the lake to await his arrival.

With a tiny twittering chitter, Joey hopped out of the lily patch and came leaping joyously toward him. Big Roo balanced imposingly on his great tail and looked down at the little leaper.

"*Chut! Ch-ch-ch!*" Joey said as the great boomer lowered his head and touched noses with him.

Then "the old man of the bush" lay down in the grass, and with a deep sigh, stretched out to rest, too tired to slake his thirst but at peace with the world.

* * * * *

"Big Roo," by Vance Joseph Hoyt. Published in The Boys' World, *March 26, 1939. Printed by permission of Joe Wheeler (P.O. Box 1246, Conifer, CO 80433) and David C. Cook, Colorado Springs, CO 80918. Joseph Hoyt Vance wrote for popular magazines during the first half of the twentieth century.*

THE KILLER'S CUNNING

Ashley G. Emmer

That a man-eating leopard was on the prowl, there could be no doubt. A big-game hunter was sent for so he could save the village people from the next attack. Instead—something else happened!

* * * * *

"Do you really mean, Captain, that the Himalayan leopard actually hypnotizes its prey?" I queried.

"Well, I use the term for want of a better one. I do know that the cold stare of Mr. *Lugger Bugger* [leopard] appears to paralyze a monkey. I once saw a poor *lungor* [monkey] in the high branches of an oak, apparently bewitched by the eyes of the killer beneath, lifeless at his feet."

"Oh, do please tell us about it, Captain Corbett," chorused the girls.

Well, we were gathered in the lounge of a small English country club in northeast India. Captain Corbett and my father had recently returned from a tiger shoot in the Terai jungles in the foothills of the Himalayas. As the two hunters and the other grown-ups strolled off the tennis courts at dusk, a number of us children had planned to waylay the captain for a tiger story.

The tall *shikari* was a good sport and fond of children. Thus it was not long before his protestations weakened, and he had permitted himself to be captured and led into a corner of the old-fashioned club parlor.

There on the four walls spread tiger, leopard, and bear skins with terrifying, snarling heads. This was just the right environment for a hair-raising jungle story, and the captain had a bulging repertoire of them.

But tonight we had allowed our hunter friend to digress from tigers to leopards. And he had even led us off unawares onto this monkey trail!

"Well, before we start this story, which will have to be positively the last for tonight, children, let us all get comfortably settled again in our chairs and cool off with an iced drink.

"Abdar," called the captain to the white-robed waiter standing by, "bring us a round of lemonades, will you? Let's have them right away."

Before many minutes passed, we were all resettled—some enviable younger creatures on the arm of Captain Corbett's divan, and others of us on the animal-skin rugs that covered the floor. But all crowded just as close as comfort and the captain would permit on this hot summer evening. Soon we had guzzled our lemonades and were sucking on the chunks of ice at the bottom of our glasses.

"As I was saying, boys and girls," continued the storyteller, "Mr. Spots likes monkey meat, and he does not waste any energy getting it once he has decided on that for a supper menu. I happened to be eyewitness to a capture that cost that fellow there his skin."

The speaker nodded in the direction of the beautiful leopard fur on which I was seated that very moment! Unconsciously I shuffled on the rug just a little bit. My friends all laughed at my expense. Then our friend continued.

"The village folk of Sherkadunda had appealed to me to rid them of a man-eating leopard that had been worrying the district for weeks. Only the night before a native child had been dragged from a mud hut. The *zamindar,* being armed with nothing but a muzzle-loader of Mutiny [against the British] days, had sent an envoy to the commissioner sahib. I set out as soon as I had arranged for the postponement of that afternoon's business engagements.

"But it was almost noon already. I was not sure that I could reach Sherkadunda before sundown. As you know, it is imperative to build one's *machan* [tree platform], tie bait, and climb into concealment at least one hour before

dark. Otherwise the human scent will hang on the moist evening air, and the animals will keep away. However, in the event of my not being able to make my objective that evening, I knew of a dak bungalow at which I could spend the night.

"So I set out from my camp headquarters. I was walking in company with my orderly and a coolie carrying my camp cot and bedding. On my way through the hills I noticed fresh pug marks crossing and recrossing the trail. In fact, later in the afternoon I'd heard a clamorous chattering of monkeys not so far away in the jungle—a sure sign that they were aware of a predaceous intruder in their feeding grounds. Apparently a leopard was stalking them in the hopes of securing a juicy morsel for his evening meal."

"Was it the man eater, do you think?" I interjected.

"No, I don't think so," explained Captain Corbett. "You see, man eaters are usually older animals that have grown too stiff to chase sprightly game, and so they resort to slower-motioned prey. No, this leopard was too young to be a man eater, as its skin readily indicates."

The fur on which I sat was soft and thick and free from scars.

"I thought no more of those monkeys at the time. I was after the man-killer, only a few miles away, and did not wish to disturb the forests and scare him away from the vicinity.

"But when I arrived at the little travelers' home that evening, the monkeys were still scolding in the adjacent forest and were shaking tree limbs noisily as though trying to frighten away some unwelcome predator.

"I decided, therefore, to go into the jungle, climb a tree, and just watch those monkeys. It was a beautiful evening, and the full moon was to rise at seven o'clock. So after paying off the coolie, I called for the watchman in charge of the cottage.

" 'What is worrying those *lungors, chowkidar?*' I asked.

" '*Lugger bugger*, sahib.' He grinned. 'Him verree bold these days, sar,' he complained in broken English. 'I see him last night. He try grab my *pariah* [low-caste native]. Leopard right by me. I hit him with *lathi* [heavy bamboo]. Him young and playful. Beootiful skin, sar.'

" 'You think I'll see the *lugger bugger*, then, if I go into the jungle?'

" 'Oah, yes, sar. He no afraid. Sahib sit and wait in tree. Lots of fun coming,' encouraged the servant with a broad smile.

" 'Very well, then. I shall spend a few hours in the forest. Have supper ready for me when I get back.'

"So saying, I hurried into the jungle with my express rifle, careful to keep on the leeward side of the monkeys, so as not to betray my presence.

"Climbing high into the leafy branches of an oak, I found a concealed perch in a triangular crotch, the upright limb of which served as an excellent back rest. Since it was some time yet before sunset, I made myself comfortable and waited.

"A little barking deer glided past my tree. But I noticed her sniff the air suspiciously and soon saw her running back from the direction in which the monkeys were jabbering."

"She must have scented the leopard!" speculated my younger brother.

"Yes, that proved to be so. For as the shadows deepened, the monkeys became even more panicky. They seemed to be coming closer to me all the time. In fact, it was not long before some of the herd swung past me, so preoccupied that they quite ignored my presence! Some even jumped into my tree, and then scampered, chattering on their way. There must have been at least five hundred beautiful silver-coated, black-faced monkeys in that herd. Some stragglers were so frightened they nearly ran into me.

"Minutes passed. The noise of the *lungors* was fading in the distance now. The whole herd had swung past, I thought. The moonlight was now piercing the lacy ceiling of the forest. I was getting ready to climb down and return to the dak bungalow and the curry and rice the cook, no doubt, had awaiting me.

"Then all at once I heard a most pitiful wail from an oak not fifty feet to my left. Having located the sound, I turned quietly. There, on about the same level as I was, was a lone monkey, cut off from the herd and crying like a baby!

"My heart was touched. From stories I had heard but never verified, I guessed what was about to happen. Was nature going to privilege me to witness a scene afforded few white men? I waited breathlessly.

"What was that noise? I heard a low sawing, as though two branches were scraping in the wind. A leopard? Where was he? Was he after me or the monkey? I hardly moved an eyelid.

"There he stood! At the foot of the very tree to which the poor monkey was clinging! The big spotted cat was as clearly visible as though he were confined within a circus arena. He was a magnificent creature. His coat shimmered in the soft moonlight. As he stared up at his quarry, his eyes closed like fireballs.

"Would the plunderer climb after the monkey? I wondered. Never before

had I experienced any such jungle proceeding as this. I had heard credulous stories from natives having to do with the leopard's so-called hypnotic gaze. Now I was to learn firsthand whether those legends had any basis in fact.

"As these thoughts raced through my mind, my eyes did not move. The leopard sat on his haunches at the foot of the tree and looked steadfastly up at his supper. Apparently he had no intention of climbing after the monkey.

"He just continued to sit and stare. In no time at all the little monkey was petrified! He seemed glued to his perch. At first he would look in every direction save the leopard's, as he sobbed piteously. I was strongly tempted to end the little fellow's torture by leveling my rifle at his inquisitor. But my curiosity got the better of me. I just waited.

"It is hard to say how many minutes my watch ticked off. I began to wonder whether the little monkey would sit in the tree all night and so foil his foe's intentions, or whether the sleek hunter might not yet climb after his prey.

"I noticed, however, that the poor monkey now seemed to be absolutely transfixed. His body was rigid, and his eyes glued upon his tormentor's. The foolish little creature had permitted his gaze to settle upon his captor's. It really did *seem* as though the leopard's eyes possessed some sort of mesmerizing power.

"Sooner than I expected the monkey's ordeal ended. With a curdling moan, the paralyzed creature thudded to earth. He had paid the supreme price for permitting himself to be cut off from his companions in the first place; and then for allowing himself to be caught in the leopard's bewitching stare.

"As the monkey fell to the ground, the bloodthirsty leopard was upon him. But a moment later his snarl turned into a death rattle as he rolled over, mortally wounded.

"My well-placed shot was too late to save the little monkey. However, the next morning I found the jungle mesmerist stretched out stiff under a berry bramble. The natives helped me skin him.

"My sympathy for the monkey had finally conquered my *shikari* sense; I never did get a shot at the man eater I was after. Fortunately, he was scared away from that neighborhood. In fact, he was never heard of again, which is unusual. He must have died a natural death in the jungle.

"Anyway, I know I brought home a better fur than he could have furnished me. And in the bargain, I had discovered another jungle secret.

"And now, children, I suppose it is time for bed. I hope you do not dream that the leopards are tracking you down tonight."

We thanked the captain heartily for his story and bade him good night. Thoughtfully we walked home across the police parade ground, one of my father's *sepoys* showing the way with a kerosene lantern, which cast uncertain, frightening shadows. The drumming of the village *pariahs* was unnerving. Captain Corbett's story had electrified our imaginations.

* * * * *

"The Killer's Cunning," by Ashley G. Emmer. Published in The Youth's In-structor, *June 6, 1944. Printed by permission of Joe Wheeler (P.O. Box 1246, Conifer, CO 80433) and Review and Herald® Publishing Association. Ashley G. Emmer wrote for mid-twentieth-century magazines.*

SOLIMIN—A CAMEL STORY FOR CHILDREN

Susan Coolidge

So what is the difference between a desert and a dessert? Did you know there exists a desert almost as big as the Atlantic Ocean? What are camels good for?

In this story about a certain camel, we can find the answers to all these questions.

* * * * *

I asked a party of children once the meaning of the word *desert,* and all but one shouted out, "Rice pudding and oranges!" having in their minds the dinner which we had just eaten. That one, who was older than the rest, said, rather shyly, "A big piece of land, Aunty, isn't it?" But even he didn't know how big—or that there is a difference in spelling between the *dessert* which people eat and the *desert* which sometimes eats people, closing its jaws of sand, and swallowing them up as easily as a boy swallows a cherry.

The biggest desert in the world is in Africa and is called the Sahara. It is almost as large as the Atlantic Ocean, but instead of water, it is all sand and rocks. Like the ocean, it is visited with storms—dreadful gales, when the wind scoops up thousands of tons of sand and drives them forward, burying and crushing all they meet. And it has islands, too—small green patches,

where springs bubble through the ground, and ferns and acacias and palm trees grow. When a traveler sees one of these fertile spots afar off, he feels as a tempest-tossed sailor does at sight of land. It is delightful to quit the hot, baking sun, sit in shadow under the trees, and rest the eyes, long wearied with dazzling sands, on the sweet green and the clear spring. Oases, these islands are called. Long distances divide them. It is often a race for life to get across from one to the other. Sometimes people do not get across! In 1805, a caravan of two thousand persons died miserably of heat and thirst in the great desert, and the sand covered them up. Do you wonder at my saying that the desert eats people?

Now, you will be puzzled to guess what sort of ship it is that swims this dry ocean. It is the camel—an animal made by God to endure these dreadful regions, in which no other beast of burden can live and travel. I dare say many of you have seen camels in menageries. They are ugly animals, but very strong, swift, and untiring. With a load of eight hundred pounds on his back, a camel will travel for days at the rate of eight miles an hour, which is as fast as a sailing ship can move. More wonderful still, he will do this without stopping for food or water. Nature has provided him with an extra stomach, in which he keeps a store of drink, and with a hump on his back, made of jellylike fat, which, in time of need, is absorbed into the system and appropriated as food. Is it not strange to think of a creature with a cistern and a meat-locker inside him? A horse would be useless in the desert, where no oats or grass can be had; but the brave, patient camel goes steadily on without complaint till the oasis is reached: then he champs his thorn bushes, fills himself from the spring, allows the heavy pack to be fastened on his back again, and is ready for further travel.

Now you know what sort of a ship it is that I am going to tell you about. It was a camel, name Solimin. He was of a rare and valuable breed, known as "herie," or coursers, because they are so much swifter than ordinary camels. Solimin's master, Ahmed, was a poor man. He never could have afforded to buy a full-grown camel of this rare breed; and Solimin had become his through a piece of good fortune. When a little foal, Solimin was found in a lonely place in the desert, standing over the dead body of his mother, who had fallen and perished along the way. Led to the brown tent which was Ahmed's home, the orphan baby grew up as a child of the family, lay among the little ones at night, and was their pet and plaything all the day. The boys taught him to kneel, to rise, to carry burdens, to turn this way and that at a signal. The girls hung a necklace of blessed shells around his neck, saved for him the best of the food, sang him songs (which he was supposed to enjoy), and daily kissed and stroked his gentle nose and eyes. As he grew big and strong, the pride of his owners grew with him. Not another family of the tribe possessed a herie. Several times, Ahmed was offered a large price for him, but he rejected it with disdain.

"Would I sell my son—the son of my heart?" he said. "Neither will I part with Solimin. By the Prophet, I swear it."

Of all the dwellers in the brown tent, Solimin loved best Ahmed himself, and his eldest son, Mustapha. With them he was docile as a lamb; but if strangers drew near, or persons he did not like, he became restive and fierce, screamed, laid back his ears, and kicked with his strong hind legs. A kick from a camel is no joke, I can tell you. All the desert guides knew Solimin, and, for his sake, Ahmed was often hired to accompany caravans. And, once, at Cairo, Solimin was chosen to carry the sacred person of the Khedive (a viceroy) on a day's excursion up the Nile bank, an honor the tribe boasted about for months afterward.

It was the year after this journey to Cairo that Ahmed met with a terrible adventure. He and Mustapha, making their way home after a long journey, had lain down to sleep away the noontide hours, according to the custom of desert travelers. Their camels were tethered beside them, all seemed secure and peaceful, when, sudden as the lowering of a cloud, a party of Arabs, belonging to a wild tribe at enmity with all men, pounced upon them. Ahmed and his son defended themselves manfully, but what could two men, surprised in sleep, do against a dozen? In five minutes it was all over. The assailants vanished in a cloud of dust, and when Ahmed, who had been struck down in the attack, recovered his senses, it was only to find camels, baggage, belt, money, everything gone, and Mustapha wounded and motionless on the earth beside him.

Ahmed thought him dead. They were alone in the desert, a hundred miles from home, without food or water; and with a groan of despair he sat down beside his son's body, bowed his head, and waited until death should come to him also. An Arab believes in fate and tends to be resigned to it when misfortune occurs.

But Mustapha stirred, and Ahmed at once sprang up. There was little he could do for the poor boy, except to chafe and rub his hands; but at least he could do *something*. Before long, Mustapha revived enough to speak.

"Are they gone?" he asked.

"Yes, the accursed ones, they are gone, with all our goods and with Solimin! The Prophet's curse light upon them!" And passing from despair to fury, Ahmed threw sand upon his head, and flung himself on the ground in helpless rage. Mustapha joined in with groans and lamentations.

When the father and son grew calmer, they began to discuss their situation. Ahmed knew of a small unfrequented oasis, about twenty miles away. It was their only chance of safety, but could they reach it?

"I *think* I can walk," declared Mustapha, tying up his wounded leg in a fold torn from his turban. But he limped sadly, and his tightly pressed lips revealed pain as he moved. He was faint with hunger beside. Neither of the men had eaten since sunrise.

Suddenly Mustapha uttered a joyful cry and lifted something from the earth.

"The Prophet be praised!" he cried. "My father, here is food. The robbers have dropped a bag of dates."

Sure enough, there it lay, a heavy bag of dates, shaken off from some camel's pack during the struggle. Heavy as it was and hard to carry, Ahmed wished it were larger yet. It staved off starvation. A handful of its contents satisfied hunger and gave them strength to begin their walk. And what a walk it was! Poor Mustapha collapsed every half-hour from pain and weakness; the sand was heavy, the darkness disoriented them. When morning broke, they'd covered barely half the distance. All through the hot daytime they lay panting on the ground, eating now and then a date, tormented with thirst and heat; and when evening came, they dragged themselves to their feet again and recommenced their painful journey. Step by step, hour by hour, each harder and longer than the last, moment by moment they grew more feeble, less able to continue, till it seemed as though they could no longer struggle on. At last, the morning broke. Ahmed raised his bloodshot eyes, seized Mustapha's arm, and pointed. There, not a hundred yards away, was the oasis, its trees and bushes outlined against the sky.

Poor Mustapha was so spent that his father had to drag him across the short dividing space. It was a small oasis and not very fertile; its well was shallow and scanty, but no ice-cooled sherbet ever seemed more delicious than did its brackish waters to the parched tongues of the exhausted men.

All day and all night they lay under the shadow of the cactuses and the acacia trees, waking only to drink, then falling asleep again immediately. Shade and sleep and water seemed the only things in the world worth having just then.

The second day they slept less, but it was nearly a week before they could be said to be wide-awake again. Such a pair of scare-crows they were! Ahmed was almost naked. The robbers had taken part of his clothes, and the desert thorns the rest. Haggard, wild, blackened by the sun, they gazed at each other with horror; each thinking, *Do I look like that?* and each tried to hide from the other his own torment.

They could never tell afterward how long they remained at the oasis. It seemed years, but it was in reality only weeks. All day long they looked wistfully toward the horizon, in hopes of a caravan, but no caravan ever came. Slowly the dates dwindled in the bag; slowly the precious water diminished in the well; a little longer, and starvation would be certain. They scarcely spoke to each other during those last days, but each sat by himself in a sort of dull despair. At night, when they fell asleep, they dreamed of food, and woke in the morning to find themselves still hungry. It was horrible!

Then came a morning when they rose to find the hard desert outline, which they knew so well, vanished and gone, and in its stead a smooth, shining lake, fringed with trees and dotted with feathery, fairy islands. So near it seemed, and so real, that it was as though they heard the ripple of the water and the rustling of the wind in the tree boughs. Mustapha stared as though his eyes would burst from his head; then he gave a wild cry and was rushing away; but his father held him fast.

"Stay, my son! Stay, Mustapha! It is no lake—it is a device of Satan. What you behold is the mirage, spread by devils for men's destruction."

"Let me go!" shrieked Mustapha, writhing and struggling.

But even as he strove, the soft water outlines shifted and trembled; the lake rose in air, melted, and sailed off into curling mists; the trees, the whole fair picture, dissolved, and the well-remembered sands and black rocks took its place. With a cry of horror, Mustapha slid through his father's arms to the earth, hid his face, and cried like a child.

Next morning, only one date was left in the bag. Ahmed put it in his son's hand with a mournful look.

"Eat, my son," he said, "eat, and then we will die. *Allah il Allah!*"

A long silence followed; there seemed nothing more to say. Suddenly, from afar off, came to their ears the tinkle of a bell.

Mustapha raised his head.

"Is it the mirage again, my father?" he asked. "For it seems to me that I hear the bell from the neck of Solimin, our camel."

Eagerly they listened. Again the bell tinkled, and, looking through the bushes, they saw, floating toward them, as it seemed, the form of a gigantic camel. Soundless and still, it moved rapidly along. Behind, but much farther away, other forms could be seen, still dim and indistinct, veiled by the mist of driving sand.

Suddenly Mustapha gave a start.

"My father," he cried, in an excited whisper, "it *is* Solimin! I am not mistaken! What other camel ever resembled Solimin? Don't you see his lofty hump, his arched neck? Doesn't the bell tinkle like the voice of home?"

Then, half rising, he gave, with what little power he had left, the well-known call.

Solimin—for it was indeed he—paused as the sound caught his ears, and sniffed the wind. Again came the call; he wheeled, plunged, threw his rider, dashed forward, broke through the bushes, and in a second was on his knees before his old master.

"Up, up, my father! there is no time to lose!" cried Mustapha, grown stronger in an instant. "Up, up! for the robbers are closing in on us!"

In fact, wild cries and clouds of dust showed that the foe had taken the alarm and were hurrying on. But already Ahmed and Mustapha were mounted, and Solimin, like a ship at full sail, was speeding away with them. And where was the camel could overtake him, even when he was loaded double? Fast and swift his long, swinging trot bore them onward, and before two hours were gone, all traces of the pursuers had disappeared behind them, and they were free to turn their course toward the brown tents where rest, and food, and welcome had waited so long for their coming, and where, after a little time, their hardships and sufferings seemed to them only like a bad dream.

As for Solimin, it would be difficult to be more tenderly treated or beloved than he'd been before this adventure; but if the freshest water, the prickliest *Khedive* furze, if bowls of sour milk, if a triple necklace of shells, if brushing and grooming, if soft pats from childish fingers, and sweet names murmured in his ears by girlish voices can make a camel happy, then is Solimin the happiest of heries. Solimin is no longer, however. His name has been changed to "The Blessed," in memory of the day when, like a stately ship, he came over the desert sea and bore his starving masters to home and life and liberty.

* * * * *

"Solimin—A Camel Story for Children," by Susan Coolidge. Published in St. Nicholas, *November 1878. Original text owned by Joe Wheeler. Susan Coolidge wrote for popular magazines during the second half of the nineteenth century.*

Rift Valley King

L. R. Cronkhite

The king of beasts knew it must come to this: fierce leopards that killed just for the sport of it had invaded his domain, and every day that passed, his cubs had less to eat.

There was no question as to if *a showdown would come; the only question had to do with* when.

* * * * *

On a rocky ledge thrust out from the mouth of a dark cavern, three baby lions tumbled about playfully. Not far away the tawny-colored body of a huge lioness was stretched lazily upon the rocks. Through half-closed eyes she watched the playful capers of her offspring with just pride at being the mother of three of the finest cubs ever born in the Great Rift Valley, Africa's game paradise.

A movement in the tall elephant grass to the left caused the lioness to become suddenly alert. With ears raised and listening she waited, her keen eyes followed a rippling weave that ran through the tall grass, coming ever closer. By means of animal communication she sent a message to her cubs, and they quickly backed into the mouth of the cave. Then from the depth of

the tall grass the head of a huge male lion appeared. He surveyed his castle home with tranquil eyes that kindled with parental affection at sight of the three cubs toddling out of the cave. Over the past four years, he and his mate had lived at the edge of the savanna near the upper end of the Great Rift Valley. Seeing her lordly mate which the natives had named Thunderbolt because of his great size and speed, the lioness again stretched out for a nap, knowing her lair was safe with him on guard.

At the approach of Thunderbolt, the three cubs ran toward him with eager expectancy, looking for the food he always brought. The savanna and nearby jungle abounded in game, and ordinarily he had no trouble in securing food, but today the great lion had found no game. He had discovered something that had both puzzled and alarmed him, however: first, he had found the scanty remains of an antelope on which some creature had dined. That might have been the work of another lion, and Thunderbolt gave it no heed. A little later, however, he had come to a spot where three bright-eyed gazelles had been slain and only one partially eaten. Instantly, he had known it was not the act of one of his kind. The king of beasts does not kill for the mere lust of killing.

Thunderbolt had sniffed at the carcasses suspiciously. There had been a strong acrid scent about the place that had aroused his resentment. He had lifted his great shaggy head and glared about. From deep in his throat had come a rumbling sound that had risen to a mighty roar. It had made the leaves tremble and sent a pair of chimpanzees scurrying high up in the tree-tops. He had sniffed again significantly. Instinct had told him this was the work of leopards.

From that time on food became scarce in the upper Great Rift Valley. The presence of those ruthless killers sent the forest dwellers fleeing to other regions; but while other creatures feared and fled, Thunderbolt raged with resentment. It was not alone that the leopards made food scarce for him and his family. Such a skillful hunter as he could surmount that difficulty. He particularly resented the encroachment of these wanton killers upon that which he considered his domain. He hated leopards for their bloodthirsti-ness. For years he had reigned over the upper Great Rift Valley, proving himself a beneficent ruler. He killed only when hunger drove him to it. His very presence in the valley had become something like that of nature's police-man. He kept out the more rapacious beasts and by his example compelled respect for the law of moderation. That such outlaws as the leopards should come and begin ruthlessly to slay in disregard of the accepted law of his do-main filled him with rage.

A few days later Thunderbolt had his first introduction to the great beasts and witnessed at a distance the evidence of their strength and ferocity. He had been driven much farther from his lair than usual in quest of game. Coming along a reed-encircled rill, he paused to rest in the shade of an acacia bush. At a water hole an eighth of a mile away, he saw a buffalo bull shamble down to the water and begin to drink. He was a splendid big fellow with thick-set body and powerful neck. Two formidable horns curved out over the broad forehead.

From out of the brushwood behind the buffalo two black forms appeared. Without noise their sinewy bodies glided over the ground toward the unsus-pecting animal. Indeed there seemed little reason for the buffalo to be on guard since few animals would dare attack him. When the black leopards were almost within striking distance, a sixth sense within the animal warned him of im-pending danger. He flung up his head with a snort and started to turn. He was too late. One great brute sprang to hamstring the buffalo while the other leaped at his throat. The struggle was terrific but brief. Before the last convulsive strug-gle was over, the two great brutes settled down to their feast.

Thunderbolt had watched the battle that cost the gallant bull his life without the outward move of a muscle, but within his brain were conflicting emotions: rage mingled with admiration for such prowess and more than a hint of fear. The fact that these relentless killers had unhesitatingly attacked the bull filled Thunderbolt with dread. Instinct told him that soon he must meet them in a decisive conflict. They might have met this afternoon had Thunderbolt so elected, for the leopards lingered long over their kill; however, he had no desire to pick a quarrel with two such beasts as the black leopards had just demonstrated themselves to be. If destiny brought the three together all well and good; but for the present, Thunderbolt was content to vent his rage in silence. Taking a shortcut for his den with a manner far from befitting the king of the Great Rift Valley, the big lion bounded away.

* * * * *

Days passed and the black leopards grew more bold in their depredations. It seemed nothing short of insolence that led them to attack a band of guenons—those expert trapeze performers of the monkey tribe—almost within a stone's throw of Thunderbolt's den. The little monkeys had chosen the place for their home because dwelling within the shadow of the great lion's cave seemed to offer security. Thunderbolt had never attacked them, and up until the coming of the black leopards no animal had ventured so near the lair.

One evening when the guenons were in the midst of one of their acrobatic frolics, two sinister shadows came stealing through the trees. Before the wary old leader realized there was danger abroad, the thing happened. Through the tree branches the two black shadows came, silent and threatening. Then with a fiendish squall, a muscular body came hurtling through the air. It landed on the old leader himself, crushing him down with terrible force. For a moment the masklike face of the leopard was pressed against the monkey while scimitar fangs closed upon his throat. Then with a swift movement the great cat flung the lifeless body of the little monkey into the bushes and leaped for another victim. Before the guenons made their escape, seven of their number fell before the leopards' merciless attack. In justice to Thunderbolt, it must be stated that he was away on a hunting trip. The scarcity of game made it necessary for him to go much farther afield than formerly. The lioness, too, was some distance away and arrived just in time to see the black leopards leap away in pursuit of the fleeing guenons.

When Thunderbolt returned and witnessed the results of that savage killing, he was furious. He roared a challenge to the leopards who were now miles away, sleeping off the effect of their gluttony. Such daring audacity perpetrated in his front yard aroused the big lion to renewed determination to vanquish the slayers. Little did he understand that the beasts, the bloodthirsty exploits of which had wrought such havoc on the forest folk, were also bent upon his own destruction.

Dawn came to the Great Rift Valley. With the morning sunlight drenching the wooded slopes, the creatures that prowl about at night slunk away into thickets or vine-covered recesses. Secure in his castle home, the king of the Rift Valley slept. For two days he had not left the lair. The reason was an injured forepaw, lacerated on a sharp stone while hunting. Early this morning the lioness had gone in quest of food for her cubs and mate.

Thunderbolt lay on a ledge of rocks trying to extend his morning nap a little longer. Three baby lions, mischievous as kittens, seemed equally determined to bring it to an end. They climbed upon his side, tumbled over his broad shoulders and at times terminated their slides by applying brakes in the form of brierlike claws. Within the tall elephant grass not far away, two mighty slayers were concealed—alert, watchful. Hunger had overtaken the black leopards, and they had returned hoping to again dine on the little guenons. They had been hunting most of the night with but little success and were in an ugly mood. Their own wanton destruction of wild game had resulted in such a depletion of the forest family that they were finding it difficult to get enough food, much less satisfy their lust for killing.

One of the big beasts lifted his head furtively. He saw Thunderbolt dozing on the ledge with the playful cubs romping over him; he snarled savagely. The other beast sighted the lion; the leopards' eyes became smouldering bits of jade-green fire. The very peacefulness of the domestic scene before them seemed to enrage the leopards to a fury. Beneath their glossy fur of midnight blackness, powerful muscles became tense as drawn steel. Their faces revealed fangs of ivory whiteness while their red tongues were flecked with foam.

While they hesitated to attack, a stray antelope came leisurely down the jungle path. Unaware of the presence of either the lion or leopards, the buck began to nibble at tufts of grass. Then Thunderbolt saw the animal and slid noiselessly from the ledge. Here was food, and he as well as the cubs was hungry. Detouring to approach from upwind, the big lion went forward with the confidence of an experienced and skillful hunter.

While he was still yards away, one of the leopards reached the antelope. With outstretched body so taut that it resembled a lance hurled from ambush, the big cat landed on the buck's back. The antelope gave a terrified bawl, reared, and sought to flee. With uncanny skill, the leopard crooked a sinewy foreleg about the buck's head and gave a sharp upward thrust. There was a dull, snapping sound, and the antelope went down without a struggle. The other leopard sprang forward, intent upon sharing the good fortune.

Before either had a chance to sample the kill, a thunderous roar rent the jungle stillness. With the speed of an express train, Thunderbolt charged. He looked upon the coming of the buck as nature's special offering, a consideration rightfully due to a king. To be cheated out of the prey was maddening.

If Thunderbolt expected the leopards to retreat before that terrifying charge, he was destined to disappointment. With fangs bared in cold ferocity the black leopards answered with a challenging squall.

Across the lifeless body of the antelope the great lion hurled himself straight at the nearest leopard. With unbelieving swiftness the big cat sprang aside. Out shot a mailed forepaw, and claws cut deeply into the lion's side. With a roar of pain Thunderbolt wheeled. He sprang to crush his antagonist, but with remarkable agility the black leopard evaded him. In that instant the other leopard sprang upon the lion's back, sinking cruel fangs into thick muscles before Thunderbolt could dislodge him.

From their place on the ledge, the cubs watched in awed amazement while their sire fought for his life. If he lost, the leopards would make short work of them.

Turning, twisting, and circling, the great beasts lunged at each other in movements too swift for the eye to follow. As yet not one of Thunderbolt's blows had landed. Whenever he sprang at one of the beasts, the other would attack him from behind. Not once but many times their terrible claws ripped his back, sides and flanks. He was covered with his own blood and breathing heavily from exertion. The fiendish squalling of the black leopards mingled with the guttural roar of the lion struck terror into the hearts of the forest creatures.

Fear-stricken, a baby lion backed into the den, whimpering. Thunderbolt, realizing he was being terribly wounded and wearing himself out, resorted to other tactics. There was a wedge-shaped notch in the rocks below the den. Feigning defeat Thunderbolt began backing toward this. Emboldened by his retreat, the leopards pressed the battle with renewed fury.

When his hind quarters touched the rocks, Thunderbolt sank down, seemingly exhausted. With a cry of rage and triumph the big cats closed in. It was a fatal mistake. Too late the foremost attacker saw this and tried to spring aside. While he was still in midair, Thunderbolt caught the leopard with a smashing blow. The force of it flung the beast into the rocks.

Before the second one had time to retreat, the great lion was upon him. A pair of tawny forearms as thick as a man's thigh encircled the black body. With irresistible force Thunderbolt thrust the leopard back while his great jaws closed upon the hateful throat.

With an appalling scream the beast that had so often slain others realized the hour of nature's retribution had struck.

Having finished with this one, the mighty lion turned to destroy the other leopard, but the terrific blow he had given the big cat made further effort unnecessary. Thunderbolt sniffed contemptuously at the limp body, then trotted toward his den. His sovereignty over the Great Rift Valley was again established. In a short time the forest creatures–guenons, giraffes, zebras, gazelles and the rest—would be returning.

Moving with majestic ease befitting a king, Thunderbolt sprang lightly to the ledge. Three frightened little cubs emerged from the cave, and three pairs of bright eyes looked with deepest awe upon their victorious sire.

Thunderbolt flung himself down to rest, turning upon them a look of parental affection which seemed to say: "Come on now and finish your frolic."

* * * * *

"Rift Valley King," by L. R. Cronkhite. Published in The Boys' World, *December 26, 1937. Printed by permission of Joe Wheeler (P.O. Box 1246, Conifer, CO 80433) and David C. Cook, Colorado Springs, CO 80918. L. R. Cronkhite wrote for popular magazines during the first half of the twentieth century.*

QUEST FOR A QUETZAL

Barbara Westphal

Growing up in Latin America, I was privileged to spend three years in Guatemala with my missionary parents. We knew the Westphals well; also Moisés Tahay.

Because the iridescent, almost mythical quetzal is Guatemala's national symbol, I yearned to actually see one. Sadly, so rare is it that I was never privileged to do so.

Just as was true of Barbara Westphal; but she was determined, no matter what the cost or how long it took, to set eyes on one.

* * * * *

My quest for a quetzal became an obsession with me. The first lost opportunity came in Mexico, when we made a horseback trip across the mountains of Chiapas. We were in the *Selva Negra,* the Black Forest, where it was possible to glimpse this rare and beautiful bird. I was tantalized by the fleeting shapes and strange calls that eluded me, but because bird watching was only a by-product of that trip, and because I was the only bird enthusiast in the group, I couldn't hold up the caravan to search for quetzals or anything else. So I jogged on, mournfully parodying to myself,

"Theirs not to reason why,
Theirs but to pass this by."

It was while spending a few months in Guatemala that our friend the *professor* whetted my desire with stories and legends about the quetzal (pronounced *ket sáhl*), the emblem of his country. Though educated and living in the capital city, Professor Moisés Tahay, principal of the mission school in Guatemala City, was himself an Indian, proud of his noble ancestry.

The Maya Quiché Indians in Guatemala, he explained, believed that every man had a *nahual,* or soul mate, in the animal kingdom. So the puma or the deer that had a special affinity for a certain person would suffer or thrive or even die according to the fortunes of the man to whom he was linked.

Tecun Uman, the last chief of the Maya Quichés, had for his *nahual* the gorgeous quetzal bird. As he led his warriors to battle against Pedro de Alvarado, his quetzal was flitting about his head. Now, Tecun Uman had never before seen a man on horseback, and when he and the Spanish conquistador met face to face, he supposed that horse and rider were one.

Aiming at the horse's heart, he shot an arrow. The horse fell, but to his consternation the man leaped from the horse. In that moment Alvarado took advantage of the startled chief and thrust his sword into the heart of the Indian. As Tecun Uman fell, the quetzal also dropped to earth, staining its shining green plumage with the blood of Tecun Uman. And that, so the legend goes, is how the quetzal got its red underparts.

The quetzal, claimed as the most beautiful bird in the Western Hemisphere, belongs in a special way to Guatemala, although it may be found in the right habitat all the way from southern Mexico to Panama. Because it usually refuses to eat and cannot live in captivity (although a few zoos now have live specimens), Guatemala chose the quetzal as the symbol of freedom. With its long graceful plumes, the quetzal adorns the coat of arms and is seen in a stylized motif on Guatemalan embroidery and in weaving designs. "The money bird," some have called it, because the Guatemalan dollar equivalent to the U.S. dollar is called a *quetzal.*

Belonging to the tropical trogon family, the quetzal (*Pharomachrus mocinno*) is about the size of a ground dove with a curving "tail" three times as long. The trailing feathers are really elongated wing coverts so that when the bird flies the fantastic plumes wave from both sides. The feathers on the crown are slightly raised, giving the head the appearance of being as round as a quetzal dollar. There are golden lights on the green head, breast, and upperparts. The abdomen is bright red and the tail is barred with black and white, like that of other trogons.

The bird builds its nest in hollow trees. Sometimes it enters the hole and leaves the lovely "tail" dangling outside. What a sight it would be to see those shining plumes apparently hanging from the side of a tree!

The *profesor* told us that the quetzal is so revered by the Indians that in some places, if it swishes across their path, they bow their heads, remove their hats, and murmur, "My lord Quetzal!" This sacred bird of the Mayas has retreated with them into the humid mountain forests, where it is seldom seen by a white man.

With the *profesor* as our guide, we visited the mountain village of Momostenango. In a rocky canyon, the Indians "Sanforize" their all-wool, handwoven blankets by dipping them first in the hot springs in the river, then in the cold current, and then patiently squeezing out the water on the rocks with their bare feet. Men, women, and babies take advantage of the moment and bathe together in Edenic innocence. As we were watching the naked brown bodies in the water, the *profesor* looked up the canyon and said, "I have seen quetzals while hiking up this ravine."

My husband saw the longing question in my eyes. "No, we couldn't take time for that now," was the answer. As usual, we just stick to a schedule. Regretfully I left Guatemala.

Then a few years later I found myself unexpectedly in Central America again. This time I determined not to leave without adding quetzal to my life list of more than eight hundred species.

In El Salvador I read that quetzals could be seen in the mountains near La Palma—and probably a real explorer *could* find them there. But when we checked in at the delightful resort cottages and I asked about a horseback ride up into the higher mountains to hunt quetzals, the answer was, *"No hay quetzales."*

My husband was making a flying trip to Miami, and I determined that instead of going with him, I would go to Guatemala by bus and hunt for quetzals. The *profesor* wrote me that I should take warm clothing, as we would probably need to spend one night in the high forest. Eagerly I sewed and purchased and borrowed till I was well outfitted. When I arrived at the home of the friends in Guatemala City who share my hobby and were to share in the quetzal expedition, they asked in surprise, "Didn't you get our telegram telling you not to come?"

Though sent several days before, the telegram had not arrived, nor did it ever put in its appearance. Guatemala was under martial law, but a state of siege was not unusual there, and I hadn't thought it would deter my friends. However, the *profesor* was adamant; he refused to go into the interior at that time. The revolutionaries were fleeing right through the chosen region, it seemed. Besides, my host was very ill in bed. Clearly, there was nothing I could do. The quetzal was eluding me again.

"Couldn't we take just a short trip?" I begged.

"Oh, yes, I can take you to see the *quetzalillo* [little quetzal]," the *profesor* assured us. "It's just like the royal quetzal except that it doesn't have such a long tail."

We knew Blake's *Birds of Mexico* listed only one kind of quetzal. Then what could the *quetzalillo* be?

My hostess went with the *profesor* and me, driving us in her Volkswagen to Momostenango. The *quetzalillo* that the spry little *profesor* located for us the next morning as we hiked up a beautiful canyon was a mountain trogon. True, it had red underparts and green upperparts, but it certainly was not a royal quetzal. Again I left Guatemala disappointed.

Spending a few months in the next-door republic of Honduras, I kept asking about quetzals until friends assured me San Juancito was the place to see them. Best of all, they said, we could drive right to the spot in our car.

The winding mountain road led to a little mining town with a deserted settlement perched on a scenic lookout. On the way the road took steep plunges at sharp corners. Some well-wishers had placed a sign in one of these frightening spots: "May God go with you, chauffeur!" Both going and returning, we had to get out and push the car toward the summit.

There was an overgrown bridle trail along the mountainside. The setting was perfect, but two expeditions failed to produce the quetzal, though they produced many a new rattle in the car. "After all, our Lark isn't a jeep," my husband reminded me, "and we aren't taking it to San Juancito any more."

"If you would come back in August, you would see how the quetzals come down the mountain and feed on the fruit of the liquidambar trees," people at San Juancito had told us. But by August we would be far away. So that was that.

We moved on to Costa Rica, and my blasted hopes sprang to life. "It's easier to see quetzals in this country than in the others," I was told. "From Costa Rica they are exported to zoos."

Birding one day on the high slopes of the Poás Volcano, we sighted blue-throated toucanets. "Where there are toucanets there can be quetzals too," the bird authority who was with us encouraged. Succeeding trips up Poás yielded no quetzals, though there were the toucanets, and there were the tree ferns—the badge of the cloud forest—and, unfortunately, there were the misty clouds too.

"You're not taking our car up that volcano again," announced my husband after having it repaired a couple of times. So ended the quest in Costa Rica.

Tourists carrying binoculars easily spot one another and need no formal introduction. So it was such a friend that told me where to see quetzals in Nicaragua. I don't even remember his name, but I did carefully write down the place he mentioned: Hotel de la Montaña, Santa María Ostuma, Matagalpa, as well as the name of the owner of the coffee plantation—Leo Salazar.

"April is the time to go," I had been advised, but it was the last day of May when our schedule allowed us to drive off the highway to Matagalpa in the hills. We were wondering how the proper habitat could be found in Nicaragua, for the route of the Pan-American Highway leaves one with the impression that the country is all desolate and barren. But just a few miles out of Matagalpa we came to the side road leading down to the hotel. Enormous trees bearded with Spanish moss framed the driveway, and suddenly we were in a high forest.

"Is it too late to see quetzals?" we eagerly questioned our host. He said the best opportunities had certainly passed, but he would talk to a guide about it.

"Things are going your way," he told us at a delicious dinner that evening. "Pedro says he saw quetzals only three days ago in the middle of the afternoon. I'll have horses here for you at one-thirty tomorrow, and Pedro will guide you."

"Oh, we shouldn't stay another day and upset our schedule—and our budget too," I sighed hesitatingly.

But this time my husband surprised me. "Let's get this quetzal hunting over with once and for all. Now we're this near, we'll stay and I'll go with you."

So the next afternoon found us on horseback in the rain forest—and it was raining—following Pedro through a thick wood. We came to a fork in the trail.

"That trail is all overgrown, but it is better for 'the birds,' but for the señora this other one is better," Pedro hesitated.

I told him this señora wanted to go wherever "the birds" might be. Accordingly, he began to hack away at the overgrowth, swinging his machete first to one side and then to the other.

"This would be better yet," he explained as he left the semblance of a trail and headed up a hill, clearing openings where there were none.

If he met someone, he would say, "Have you heard 'the birds' today?" The friend would tell him just when and where he had seen them last.

From time to time he stopped, and as we waited silently, he would imitate their whistle, a short pair of phrases, one ascending and one descending. In vain we listened for an answer in the mist.

"These *animales* are very shy," he said. "I'll tell you what: you come back next April and I'll practice my whistle some more, and then we'll see them."

"It's now or never," we told him. "Let's try a little longer."

All we could hear was the *cra-a-ank, burp, burp, burp, burp*! of the three-wattled bellbird. The *ranchero*, as Pedro called him, was constantly making himself heard overhead, but never a glimpse did we catch of that white bird.

We stopped at a clearing, dismounted, and admired a corresponding clearing in the sky. Then we heard it: a sweet, faint whistle for so large a bird. Our eyes were fixed on the treetops. Looking for a green bird in a green tree can be most baffling. If the quetzal didn't have the bright-red underparts, Pedro assured us, it would be almost impossible to sight it.

Luck was with us at last—and after searching in Mexico, Guatemala, El Salvador, Honduras, and Costa Rica, we saw the quetzals in that forest in Nicaragua. From tree to tree they flew, waving their curving plumes in glittering pride. My quest for a quetzal was ended.

No, not quite. Now I want to go back and see them again!

* * * * *

"Quest for a Quetzal," by Barbara Westphal. Published in The Youth's Instructor, *September 20, 1966. Printed by permission of Joe Wheeler (P.O. Box 1246, Conifer, CO 80433) and Review and Herald® Publishing Association. Barbara Westphal, prolific author of stories and books, wrote during the middle of the twentieth century.*

THE JAGUAR AND THE CAYMANS

Robert Wilson Fenn

So if a jaguar seeks to cross a river teeming with hungry alligators, is crossing the river then an impossibility?

* * * * *

Among the curious doings of animals I have seen, none interested me more than that observed by me one night on the banks of the upper Magdalena River in Colombia, South America. We were camped on the margin of a little creek not far from where its waters mingled with those of the river, and at a point far from any villages or houses.

We had finished our evening meal, and I was enjoying my customary smoke under the *toldilla,* or netting, and chatting with my Indian companions, when, suddenly, the most awful series of catcalls that I had ever heard disturbed our peace and the night air. A prolonged yowl, like the united voices of all the cats on all the roofs of a large town, made the cold chills creep up and down my spine and gooseflesh to run all over me.

"What is it?" I asked one of the men. "*El tigre, señor* (The tiger, sir!)," he replied. "*Va a pasar el rio* [He is going to cross the river]."

"Let him cross if he wants to," said I. "But why does he want to upset my

supper and spoil my after-dinner smoke with his hideous noise?"

"Come and see, señor," he replied, and, taking up his gun, motioned me to follow him. Softly we crept along the margin of the creek toward the river, and making our way through the spines of the overhanging bamboos, came out upon the narrow beach near the mouth of the creek.

Sure enough, by crawling cautiously along in the shadow of the bluff, we saw our musical friend squatted on his haunches, with head thrown back and mouth open, emitting the most blood-curdling serenade one could ever expect to hear, and looking for all the world like a gigantic tabby cat. But what connection such a noise could have with his passage of the river I failed to see.

"Anastasio," I said in a whisper, "doesn't the foolish fellow know that he will draw all the alligators together, and when he gets into the water, he will swim off in sections?"

"Leave him alone," chuckled the Indian. "He knows how to get across." So, crouching down in the bushes on the bank of the river, we waited for his next move. I think we must have been there about twenty minutes or half an hour, and I was becoming almost worn out by the attacks of the mosquitoes, when the concert suddenly ceased. At the same moment the moon came out clear and bright from behind a cloud, and Anastasio, nudging my arm, pointed to the surface of the water in front of the jaguar. At first I thought there were a number of sticks in the water, but as the current was swift and they were motionless in their places, I was for a moment puzzled.

"*Caymanes* [alligators]," whispered the Indian, and I saw that his eyes were better than mine. There were the ugly snouts of half a dozen of the big fellows, some well out of water, and some just showing their nostrils and the bumps over their eyes, but all ready for their expected prey.

But they were to be disappointed this time; for the jaguar, immediately upon the conclusion of his serenade, started off upstream as hard as he could run along the bank of the river, and when he had gone about five hundred yards, dropped softly into the water and swam safely across, while his baffled enemies were unable to make fast enough time upstream against the swift current to get him.

I had been so interested in watching this little performance that my chance for a shot was gone, but, in fact, I hardly begrudged a whole skin to such a clever trickster.

What I cannot yet understand is how the jaguar learned to do this. Did he reason it out, or did his mother teach it to him as she had learned it by seeing some relative dragged down by the hungry jaws of the alligators? I subsequently learned that it was quite a common trick with the jaguars, although it is seldom any human being is ever privileged to see it happen. I wouldn't have seen it had it not been for Anastasio.

* * * * *

"*The Jaguar and the Caymans,*" *by Robert Wilson Fenn. Published in* St. Nicholas, *May 1898. Original text owned by Joe Wheeler. Robert Wilson Fenn wrote for turn-of-the-twentieth-century magazines.*

CHAO CHAHNG AND THE MAN EATER

Clarence Pullen

"An elephant never forgets," it is often said. A certain fierce Siamese tiger had audaciously leaped upon the back of Chao Chahng and torn the elephant's mahout from his back, never to be seen again.

But the tiger, having once tasted human flesh, had no intention of leaving the area. What happened next—well, that's Pullen's story.

* * * * *

Anyone who thinks the elephant a slow, clumsy beast would have cause to change his opinion on seeing him at work along the rivers of northern Siam (Thailand). The rainy season, which begins in April, is the time when the teak logs, cut during the dry season in the forests along the upper waters of the Menam River, are floated down to Rahang, where they are caught and rafted to Bangkok. Instead of red-shirted, spiked-shoed "river-drivers" such as handle the logs in their downstream journey to the sawmills on the Penobscot and Kennebec in Maine, the "lumber-driving" of the Siamese rivers is done by barefooted, half-naked men on elephants, and the "bone" labor and much of the thinking involved in the operation are done by the elephants.

The middle of June, some years ago, found the drive of teak logs that I was

taking down the Me-ping River about halfway on its journey from the cuttings to Rahang. My crew consisted of twenty elephants with their Shan and Lao mahouts, or keepers, who drove the logs, and as many bullock-drivers, choppers, and men-of-all-work to attend to the camps and haul supplies. Boats were needless, for there was no water too deep or current too strong for the elephants, who went up and down the steepest slopes and over rocks like great cats as they patrolled the river, rolling into the current with heads, trunks, and tusks the logs stranded along the channel, or wading out into cataracts to break a forming jam. All these elephants were tuskers, except my riding elephant, Lala, and the biggest and strongest and most docile of all was Prahada's elephant, Chao Chahng, the chief, who stood ten feet high at the shoulder. Prahada was a northern Lao, a thorough *maw chahng,* or elephant-master, who, like all good mahouts, was on the best of terms with his animal, and I had learned that the two were to be depended upon to carry through the hardest jobs that by any chance might come up in the day's work.

In camping in the forest, it was not unusual for us to find, of a morning, the tracks of some wild animal which had reconnoitered the camp during the night. Such a discovery excited no particular alarm, as the prowling beasts of Siam commonly avoid man, and the worst that was looked for from a tiger or panther was that he might spring upon a straying buffalo or goat. Hence it was the unexpected which happened, when a tiger one evening, with the whole camp awake, seized a man who had gone a few steps from one of the fires to fetch wood to replenish it. At his outcry and the sound of the tiger's growl, the Shans and Laos, realizing at once what was to be done, caught blazing brands from the fire and rushed to their comrade's rescue. A brand flung at the tiger struck him in the head, causing him to drop the man and sneak away in the darkness. The tracks of the tiger showed him to be a very large as well as bold one; but after his experience with the firebrand, he was not likely, so the men assured me, to venture into the camp again while fires were burning there. The man was not dangerously hurt, and we hoped that our troubles from wild beasts were ended, as they had begun, with this visit.

But we were not to be rid of the tiger so easily. He was lurking along our line of work on the river next day, as the alarm shown by the elephants on several occasions testified. When night came on and most of the men and elephants were back in camp, Prahada, who had been sent that day far upstream, had not returned. Presently the crashing sound of an elephant coming at full speed was heard in the forest, and soon Chao Chahng appeared in a state of great excitement, and Prahada was not on his back. He halted among the other elephants, and then we saw that his back was torn by a tiger's claws. I made up a searching-party, and by the light of torches we went back over the elephant's trail for half a mile. Then rain began to fall, ending our search, as it blotted out the tracks, and we returned, having found no sign of Prahada.

The story of the tragedy we never learned except as it was written in the wounds on Chao Chahng's back. The claw marks showed that the tiger had leaped on him from behind, and, as was to be expected, he had run away, for an attack from that quarter will throw the bravest and steadiest elephant into an uncontrollable panic. Whether Prahada slipped to the ground, was pulled down from his seat by the tiger, or was brushed off by the big elephant's running under a tree could only be guessed at, for no trace of him was ever found. That the tiger which killed and carried him off was of uncommon fierceness was shown by his leaping upon an elephant so formidable in size as Chao Chahng.

There was reason to fear that the big elephant, having felt the tiger's claws, and missing the mahout to whom he was accustomed, might refuse to work again on the river; but Prahim, a cousin of Prahada, took Chao Chahng out next day with the others and put him through his tasks without trouble. It was evident that the great creature mourned for his dead master, as was shown by his restlessness at night and by his utterance of a moaning sound from time to time, very different from the grunt and snort of the other elephants. That the great, patient creature was to be the avenger of his slain master no one in the camp could have thought or dreamed.

The tiger gave no further sign of his presence either by day or night about the camp, where, for precaution, fires were kept burning from sunset to daylight. The following day some of the elephants working above the camp showed fear of something that they saw or scented in the undergrowth on the river bank; but as I sent them out now in companies of three together, the tiger, if he was lurking about, did not venture to attack any of them. But he prowled near the camp that night, as we saw by his tracks next morning.

"Today—one, two, three since Prahada went," said a Lao forester to me, holding up his fingers one after another to signify the lapse of days; and shaking his head gloomily, he added: "Now the tiger will come back again."

After the recent tragedy, with the knowledge that the tiger which carried Prahada off was awaiting his chance for the next victim, it was a matter of course that both elephants and men should become demoralized and that work should lag. Several of the men, two with elephants, quit my service under various pretexts, but really from fear of the tiger, and I knew that if another man were carried off by him it would mean a general stampede of my force. With the purchasing firm at Bangkok impatiently awaiting the news of the arrival of the logs at Rahang, I had to see my work hindered and in danger of coming to a standstill through one murderous brute, which could not be killed or frightened away, unless by some accident, which was not at all likely. I carried my repeating-rifle on my trips from the camp, partly in the hope of catching a "snap-shot" at the tiger, but more to inspire my men with courage and confidence; and further to inspirit them I added fowls to their ration of rice, made presents of fancy cloths and tobacco to the subforemen, and promised that every elephant-driver should receive five silver coins beyond his stated pay if the logs were all down at Rahang by the first day of July.

The tail of the drive was lodged at some rapids five miles up the river, and by clearing these it would be practicable to move camp a day or two later, which might take us below the ranging of the tiger, who had made his presence known to us in every instance from somewhere above the camp. None of the men or elephants liked to be sent in this direction, and so for this work, on the third day, I detailed four of the best tuskers and driver, and accompanied them on my riding elephant. My presence, with the rifle slung to my riding-pad, gave courage to the men, which was imparted to their elephants, and they worked so well that by the middle of the afternoon the rapids were cleared.

Below the rapids the river broadened into a long pool a quarter of a mile wide, and of a depth of three or four feet except where the current had cut a deep channel along the foot of the high eastern bank. At the edge of the rapids on the east side, as I waited for Chao Chahng to push the last log into the current, I called to the three mahouts across the stream to keep on down the west bank, intending myself to take a forest path leading to the foot of the pool on the east. They had disappeared round a bend in the shore, and Lala was leading the way up the east bank from the river, when my rifle slipped from its slings and fell upon the rocks. At his mahout's command, Chao Chahng, coming on behind us, picked it up with his trunk and passed it back to me, when I found that the hammer was jammed by the fall and so would not work. We got upon the high ground, and I was hoping as we went on that the tiger would not take this time to show himself, when we heard the three elephants across the river all trumpeting together. Something in their note our animals seemed to understand, for at the sound Lala opened out her ears like fans and quickened her pace, and I could hear the big elephant gathering speed behind her. Another minute and Chao Chahng, acting as if he were beyond all control of his mahout, rushed past us and soon was lost to view among the trees ahead.

Suspecting the cause of the trumpeting, I told my mahout to keep as close after Chao Chahng as he could, and we hurried along until, in making a cut-off from the path, we came in view of the river, and the mahout, bringing Lala to a sudden halt, pointed with his hand out upon the pool. Above the surface near the opposite bank was the black-and-yellow head of a swimming tiger, the ripples of his wake widening back to the low, wooded shore, while after him into the water came the three elephants with their mahouts urging them on. They had discovered the tiger crossing the river, and knowing that in the water he was helpless to attack them, the mahouts had not hesitated to put their elephants at him. The tiger, realizing his disadvantage, was swimming fast for the eastern bank, with excellent prospects, as far as we could see, of making it safely, for Lala was of no use against him, and Chao Chahng, who might possibly have headed him off in the water, had run away.

With my rifle useless and believing that Lala would bolt as soon as the tiger touched the shore, I was thinking of following the big elephant's example, when I heard him coming back. He had been running, not from fear, but to search out a place where he could get down to the water without breaking his neck, and now he emerged from the woods at the brink of the high bank in line with the course in which the tiger was swimming. He advanced, testing his footing, until the dirt at the edge, crumbling under his feet, began to rattle down to the water; then stretching both fore legs straight out before him, he curved his big body over the brink, and went sliding down the slope. The tiger, seeing him coming, turned back toward the middle of the stream. The bank fell fifty feet down to the water, and was very steep, and how Chao Chahng avoided turning a somersault or two on the way is a mystery; but somehow he kept right side up, and, with Prahim hanging desperately to the girth to save himself from dropping over his head, he plunged into the water. From a fountain of mud and spray his trunk emerged, and then the top of his back, moving out into the river, with the mahout climbing to his place on the neck. Like a monitor in a running tide the elephant propelled himself across the deep channel, and, gaining his footing in the shallower water beyond, he loomed up, confronting the tiger, which turned and swam to a great boulder that rose some three feet above the water's surface and scrambled upon it. Here he bristled and roared, while the four elephants came up and lined themselves around him. At my command, the mahout turned Lala back toward the cataract, and fording the river there, forced her out into the pool above the other elephants, where she took a position from which I could see all that went on.

Had my rifle been in working order I could have settled matters with the tiger where he stood, for no hunter could have asked for a surer shot than he presented. With my rifle disabled the situation was quite another thing. On the rock the tiger stood level with the shoulders of the elephants, and for them to close in upon him where his spring would land him squarely upon the nearest one's head was too much to expect of elephants or mahouts. From a safe distance away they trumpeted and threatened him with their trunks, but came no nearer, while the tiger, facing one and another in turn, made feints of springing upon each, but refused to quit the rock. Even Chao Chahng, who plainly was there for business with the tiger, was not disposed, with the scratches still fresh on his back, to give him a second chance to find a foothold there. And all the while we were so near the tiger that I could see the line of singed hair along his head where the firebrand had struck when he tried to carry away the man at the camp a few nights before.

After a half-hour of waiting, with nothing gained, I was debating with myself whether a fire-raft would be more likely to dislodge the tiger than to stampede the elephants, when the muddy water grew more turbid, and I could see that it was rising around the rock. A rainfall somewhere up the river was the cause of the change, which might indicate a trifling rise or a sweeping freshet. The elephants already were quite deep in the pool, and if the water kept on rising it was certain that they would not stay until it was high enough to force the tiger from the rock. In five minutes, however, the water had risen a foot, and the elephants now were looking anxiously from the tiger up to where the rapids were beginning to roar with the coming flood. Every tropical beast stands in supreme dread of an inundation, and the tiger turned from his besiegers to sniff and growl in a new key as the roar of the cataract grew louder and the rising water washed up against his paws. With the stream surging against their shoulders, the elephants shifted about in their tracks so as to face the current, and the mahouts had to keep up a continual shouting, and work their great-toes vigorously against the backs of the flapping ears, to prevent the uneasy animals from returning to the shore. Only Chao Chahng held his ground, facing the tiger, while Lala, shuffling round uneasily, seemed undecided as to whether her safer course were to remain under his protection or to take to her heels.

Something drifted past me toward the rock—a great teak log that the rising water had brought down from somewhere upstream. As it scraped along the rock the tiger several times seemed on the point of stepping upon the log. He hesitated, but just as its rear end was passing, he glided upon it. The heavy log, floating deep in the water, sank lower beneath his weight as, crawling to the middle of it, he was borne from the rock. While the other mahouts vainly tried to force their elephants to the log, Chao Chahng, at Prahim's word, pushed swiftly forward upon the tiger, who, balancing himself upon his unsteady support, could move only forward or backward. At sight of the tusks and upraised trunk above him, the tiger, turning, with a whine of fear crept swiftly back on the log, evidently hoping to regain his place on the rock. But Chao Chahng, following his movement, struck him a sweeping side blow with his trunk that sent him flying into the water. The other tuskers, no longer to be restrained, were plunging for the shore, and Lala bolted after them. I caught one glimpse of the big elephant rushing upon the tiger struggling at the surface, and after that, while Lala took the rocks and holes at the bottom, I was kept too busy holding myself by the ropes to the pad to turn my head until we were at the shore. Then, looking back, I saw the water swirling over the rock, and above the surface only the floating log, and Chao Chahng stalking shoreward through the flood with the air of having just discovered that the river was rising.

We made our way down the shore to the camp, where the men, on learning that the man eater was killed, built bonfires in rejoicing, and, to the accompaniment of flute and pipe, sang songs for half the night in celebration of Chao Chahng and his victory over the tiger. The river rose five feet in an hour, and when it had subsided next day the tiger's body was found a mile below the pool, stranded on a bar. It had been too long in the water for the skin to be worth saving, but I wore one of his claws on my watch-guard at Rahang on the Fourth of July, which day found our camp there, with all the logs in boom, ready for rafting.

* * * * *

"Chao Chahng and the Man Eater," by Clarence Pullen. Published in St. Nicholas, *October 1904. Original text owned by Joe Wheeler. Clarence Pullen wrote for turn-of-the-twentieth-century magazines.*

Lorita, the Gadabout Parrot

Joseph Leininger Wheeler

Out of the mists of my childhood, the image of a gregarious parrot is so indelibly impressed on my mind that her memory bullheadedly refuses to remain buried in my subconscious, but continually pops up like an obstreperous telemarketer refusing to accept No as No. Her name was Lorita.

We were living in Panama when I first set eyes on her; back then she was little and cute, no larger than a small parakeet. Once I'd seen her, I began making life miserable for my parents, telling them ad nauseum that Lorita would be no trouble at all to them, for I promised to faithfully take care of the little parrot's every need. Eventually, sensing they'd have no peace unless they gave in to my nonstop importunings, Dad and Mom gave in—and Lorita became part of our lives.

One of my folks's worst fears soon became glaringly apparent: parrots rarely shut up. In size, Lorita grew and grew, as did her bilingual vocabulary. As for her voice, alas for pre-Lorita serenity! It was anything but soothing. In fact, it was both raucous and rasping, impossible to confuse with anyone else's. She chattered incessantly (except when we covered her cage at night and she mercifully became silent). Most of the time, however, she was free to move around. Clipping one wing kept her from flying very far away because that so handicapped her she could fly only in circles—when her flights began carrying her farther and farther away, out would come the clippers again.

Though she delighted in carrying on rather wacky conversations with us, she really didn't need us, for she was more than adequate company for herself. All day long we could (let me rephrase that: *could* is the wrong word because we had no option but to listen to her) hear her incessantly chattering away with herself—chortling, laughing, cackling at her own witticisms.

Initially, she loved to ride around on our fingers, but before long she grew too big and heavy, so we'd have to carry her around on our hands or shoulders. However, as she got older, she became more temperamental: if she was in the right mood, she'd quickly sidle on to a finger and ride around wherever we took her; if she was not in the mood, she'd peck the proffered finger instead. Those pecks were considered cute when she was but a small birdling, but when she reached adult size, those nips *hurt*!

Often she'd fly to us unannounced, landing either on our shoulders or, more disconcerting, on our heads, flapping wildly until she dug her claws into our scalp long enough to gain a satisfactory toehold. Then she'd joyously ride around wherever we went, occasionally taking a swipe at the nearest ear. We learned to dread her moving away from an ear, for the mere sight of that tempting target inevitably aroused every malicious thought in her greenish-yellow head.

But as much as we feared her beak, we feared her incontinence more: what food went into one end of her ran through her with astonishing speed (making us wonder if she had a bomb chute rather than a digestive system). First thing we knew, we'd feel that warmness splat on our backs, then run down to decorate shirt and pants. Just as bad would be the irrepressible cackles of the watching family. Needless to say, Mom was not amused, for the burden of washing out the nasty stains fell on her. To Lorita, however, it was as funny as it was to those who safely watched it happen to others. Indeed, all life was funny to her.

Drama in the skies

But then came the news: our family would be moving to Guatemala. What would happen to Lorita? The mere thought of having to leave Lorita behind all but broke my heart. Mom and Dad, for reasons known only to them, were disgustingly chipper. In retrospect I've sometimes suspected that

the mere thought of leaving Lorita behind validated the call to Guatemala as being a heaven-sent opportunity to once again have peace and serenity in their home.

But alas for their hopes! John Brown (the jovial president of the church's Central American operations) traveled a great deal, both by Jeep and by plane. Being both a lover of animals and a practical joker, he often smuggled pets aboard aircraft (there were no body scanners in those days) by stuffing them into small canvas sacks, attaching the sacks to his belt, then hiding the stowaways under his capacious coat. Since he also loved to eat, the extra bulk wasn't obvious to pilots and stewardesses (rarely did we see stewards on planes in those days). So Pastor Brown dashed my folks's fond hopes by regaling us with stories of his illicit breaking of Pan American World Airways strict regulations where animals were concerned. To me, Pastor Brown's stories added up to an answer to my prayers. To my much more straitlaced and ultra-conscientious father, to whom circumventing regulations was almost as wicked as breaking laws, it was an entirely different story. And Dad most certainly did not volunteer to sacrifice comfort (in that tropical heat) by hiding Lorita under a coat himself; he must have felt he was home free, for I certainly wasn't bulky enough to pull off such a thing. But Dad had failed to reckon with Pastor Brown's ingenious solution: "Oh, Larry . . . no problem! Just let Joey stuff Lorita in a shoe box, tie a string around it, bore a little airhole in the box, and carry it on board. Piece of cake."

Dad must have thought, *Get thee behind me, Satan!* But he didn't say it out loud, because Elder Brown was his boss whether he remained in Panama or moved to Guatemala. Even so, I wonder if Dad wouldn't have found valid reasons for refusing to permit me to bring Lorita along had not his soft-hearted wife taken pity on her boy and sided with Pastor Brown.

And so it came to pass that one sizzling day our family of four climbed up that long flight of movable stairs to just behind the cockpit of the gleaming silver DC-3 airliner. I can still remember how long and dark and steep it looked once we made it to the top, entered, and looked down to the back of the plane. No one stopped me, even though Mom has since then said, "Joe's face looked as guilty as if he'd just robbed a bank!"

We found our seats, strapped on our seat belts, and gazed apprehensively at the dark brown barf bags conspicuously ensconced in their pockets in front of every passenger. We'd already learned one sad truth: the DC-3s couldn't fly high enough to clear black thunderclouds, but rather were forced to fly through them. Thus the passengers had to endure the planes bucking like out-of-control broncos, being hit by lightning, and dropping in free fall thousands of feet in what were euphemistically called "air pockets." When the plane finally hit bottom, it was like hitting a wall (amazing that the wings didn't break off!). Everything that wasn't bolted down came loose, and even some overhead compartments would pop open and disgorge their contents. All the while, stomachs would be emptying into those now bulging barf bags. Little wonder we had such mixed feelings about long flights in those days!

How different prop-travel was from today's jets! First one great engine would catch, and the propeller roar into life; then the other would join in. Louder and louder, faster and faster, until the entire plane would shudder— then, the sound would decrease, we'd slowly move down the runway to our turning spot, turn, face the take-off runway, and the engines would roar again. At last we moved faster and faster down the runway until that giant sigh of relief when the nose would finally lift.

But on this particular segment of our flight from Panama City to Guatemala City (with stops in Costa Rica, Nicaragua, Honduras, and El Salvador), for some time there would be no thunderstorms, hence little turbulence. So quiet was it that it had also remained deathly quiet in the shoe box. I began to fear that poor Lorita might have suffocated to death, so I attempted to peer in through the small airhole, but all I could see was a motionless mass of yellow-green feathers. Now I *was* worried. Feeling I just had to know the worst, I untied the string, raised the box to face level so I could peer in, then (ever so slowly and gently) I raised one corner of the cardboard lid far enough so I could see in. *Then it happened!*

I'd known Lorita was a strong bird, but never until that moment had I realized just *how* strong! Inside her box, sensing deliverance from her cramped quarters at last, she flexed her muscles like so may steel springs and catapulted out of her box, wings flapping wildly, and soared out into the not-so-friendly skies (at least to screeching parrots) of Pan American World Airways. And she was anything but quiet at showing her outraged! I can hear her yet, that *S-q-u-a-w-k! S-q-u-a-w-k! S-q-u-a-w-k!* as she flew up, then swooped down, veering in every direction, taking swipes at heads as she went by. And compounding the hubbub, an eleven-year-old-boy frantically racing up and down the aisle, yelling for her to stop! After what seemed like forever but was quite likely only a matter of minutes, I caught the enraged bird, was badly clawed for my efforts, stuffed her back in the shoe box, and with trembling hands retied the lid on; all the while she frantically battled to maintain her momentary freedom.

At this juncture, one of the pilots popped out of the cockpit to see what all the hubbub was about. There was only silence. The poor fellow vainly walked up and down the aisle seeking the source of all the racket. All he could see were passengers and stewardesses with their hands over their mouths to stifle their mirth. Finally, he surrendered to their refusal to blab on me and sulkily retreated to the cockpit.

Not until we disembarked in Guatemala City did I dare untie that string and let Lorita out.

Guatemala life

Lorita quickly acclimated to city life in Guatemala City. No more was she permitted the freedom of out-of-doors. But she was surrounded by the same family—with one exception: a little baby named Marjorie was born and would revel in Lorita's nonstop monologues.

There was one compensation that her sharp eyes and fertile little brain studied surreptitiously: the open patio in the middle of the house. There was a great bougainvillea that thrived there, so much so that Dad had to keep pruning it lest it cover up the upstairs patio where Mom would dry our clothes.

Then one never-to-be-forgotten day, Lorita just disappeared! Even though we searched every possible hiding place in the house, there was no trace of her. Nor was she anywhere in the vicinity of the upstairs patio. Finally Mom sent me outside to check the neighboring streets. No Lorita. That left one final option: I started knocking on all the doors of our neighbors' homes. *"No, su pajaro no esta aqui!"* But just when I was about to give up, I struck pay dirt: here came a maid with Lorita ensconced on a broom handle.

That proved to be but the beginning of her peregrinations. Once in a while we'd catch her in time as she reached up to the top of the next step with her beak, pulled herself up, then repeated the process enough times that she'd finally reach the upstairs patio—all the while, she'd be jabbering non-stop. From there, she'd climb onto the tile roof and sashay out to one of the neighboring open patios, climb down that neighbor's steps to the lower patio—and visit. It didn't do any good to blockade our steps: she'd just climb the bougainvillea!

We ceased to worry about her; as soon as she wore out her welcome, there'd be loud clangs from the brass clapper on our front door, and there, riding in state on a broom handle, would be Lorita, glad to get home again without any further effort on her part.

* * * * *

Years passed, but Lorita's pattern of life remained the same, including her continual gaddings about. Finally, we moved again—this time to the Dominican Republic (after a much-needed furlough in the United States). This time, it was all but impossible to take Lorita with us—but, not to worry, each neighbor by then felt her to be part of the family. So Lorita stayed in that block she so loved.

I've often wondered how long she lived on. Parrots are such long-lived birds (some live sixty to eighty years) it's not impossible that even now she's climbing a set of stairs to a second-story patio, muttering, cackling, chuckling, talking, and laughing to herself: *"Pajaro bonita." "Ha-ha-ha-ha-ha." "Mar-jee! Where are you?"* Chuckle chuckle. *"Jo-eee!"* Mumble mumble. *"Ro-leeto!* [my brother Rollo Romayne]." Mumble mumble. Surprisingly, given how often we'd vainly say it, she never added, "Now, don't poop on me!" But she often chortled what we said next: *"Bad bird! Ha-ha-ha-ha-ha. Bad bird!"*

* * * * *